Love without Limits

The Secret Life of a Hospice Volunteer

By

William James Roop, M.A.B.S.

First book of the series

Kindle Direct Publishing

September 2019

Copyrighted

ISBN Number 9781692837150

This book is dedicated to my parents,

Gerald Lee Roop

Bernadine Rose Roop

who have loved and supported me all of my life.

Love without Limits

Edited by

Bernadine Rose Roop

William Roop, M.A.B.S., is a diligent student of the Bible. His exemplary research, and faithful attendance to Seminary classes has served him well. He is an avid listener, and deep thinker. In today's distracted culture the Biblical admonition, "Hear oh Israel" is seemingly ignored by the masses, but not so by Teacher William Roop. We look forward to reading more good works forged in the flames of faithfulness to Apostolic truth.

In highest regard,
Dr. Bruce A. Klein, Th.D.
Professor Dana D. Klein, M.Div.
Apostolic Theological Seminary
www.atseminary.com

Other published works by William James Roop, M.A.B.S.:

Book: The Basics of Biblical Hermeneutics. Kindle Direct Publishing. April 2019.

Book: Apostolic Church History, Volume 1. Kindle Direct Publishing. April 2022.

Book: Apostolic Church History, Volume 2. Kindle Direct Publishing. July 2022.

Blog: Hospice Care and Dying
www.hospiceministryvolunteer.blogspot.com

Blog: The Bible and Life
www.biblicalhermeneuticsposts.blogspot.com

Blog: The Trucking Tango
www.trucksandbanjos.blogspot.com

Videos: YouTube Channel Bible studies.
"Brother Roop teaches the Bible"

Videos: YouTube Channel RV Ministry
"Bill & Gretchen's Tin Can"

Videos: YouTube Channel for
Apostolic Church History
"Brother Roop"

Table of Contents

Introduction- page 11

Love Stories- page 13
My husband is in the room!
It was love at first sight
A wonderful wedding
They eloped
He whistled at her
He had been her whole life!
I was the lucky one!

Ghost Stories- page 33
My ghost story
Men with clipboards
The white-haired boy and a baby
The blue people
Too many patients See things!
The girl by the door
Ice cream with his brothers

War Stories- page 51
Vietnam or Jail
The B-17 gunner
Pearl Harbor survivor
The switchboard operator
The escape
10th mountain division
A sickness that saved him

Spiritual Stories- page 75
The prayer

Some Bible reading
Memorial Day kiss
I'm not ready to go!
The Book of John
Action ministries
Miracle on the sea

Around the Hospice- page 93
Holocaust Museum
Christmas Decorations
A Morning Walk in the Garden
The Angel with a Guitar
The Overcoming Volunteer
Nurses Helping Each Other Out
The great mule story

Stories of Compassion- page 109
His sister called
100 Years
Those don't need to be closed!
Memories of a mentor
Light complaining Is good
Two patients pass on!
Hospice pain

Stories about the Babies- page 127
Goodbye sweet little baby
Baby rocking
Baby strolling
The untouchable baby
Monday baby time
A baby forever
Love without limits

Diversity of Life- page 143
The Trucker
The Korean man
The Chinese translator
The Persians
The Czech
The Seamstress
The Oil worker
The Wanderer
The bloodhound trainer
Cocaine and needles

Poems- page 171
A windy night
Frustration
For the sake of the rose
The rest of the way
God's Love

Stories of Human Struggles-page 183
The flowers were now blooming
Indiana orphanage
A troubled man
Still going strong
Control!
Sadness overcame by joy
I have lived a hard life!

About the author- page 203

Notes- page 205

Introduction

Life in today's world is undignified! This world will chew you up and spit you out! If this does not happen to you then consider yourself blessed. If hospice is done right, using people with a special talent for compassion, they can create an oasis in someone's last days. A small oasis of dignity in this large, undignified world. I have been blessed to be a very small part of creating this oasis. For that I will be forever grateful!

Occasionally, someone will ask me why I am a hospice volunteer. It's because, when I am serving others at hospice, I feel that I am the very best human being that I can be! I have been a hospice volunteer for ten years. Becoming a hospice volunteer was probably the best decision that I have ever made. It has given me the opportunity to serve others. I have learned that the key to happiness in life is to focus your attention away from yourself. We can do that by refocusing are attention to the service to others.

The stories that I have compiled in this book are not my own. They are the stories that I have heard, or seen, in my ten years of hospice service. They are the stories of the patients, family members, nurses, volunteers and other hospice workers. I am just telling their stories, in and around our hospice.

The subtitle of this book is called "The secret life of a hospice volunteer." I subtitled it that way because many of the experiences are between the patient and the volunteer. When the patient dies, then the volunteer is left with that intimate story, or experience. That story is imbedded into the spirit of the volunteer for the rest of their life. It becomes kind of a secret.

All of these stories have come directly from my hospice blog. As a farmer surveys the countryside, he chooses which crop he will plant in which field. In this practical way, I have picked which stories to share with you. My goal is to plant these stories in the fields of my readers.

All names have been changed, or not mentioned at all, in order to protect the privacy of the people in their stories. Fictitious names have been used throughout the book. Privacy is important to all of us. So, if you read a lot of "the patient" or a lot of "he" or "she" words, please forgive me. The hospice where I volunteer at is only referred to as "our hospice." Again, that is for privacy of our hospice.

The best way to read this book is to read one of the stories, then take some time to think about it, and take a small emotional break, then you can read another one.

Love Stories

My husband is in the room!

I was at the hospice volunteering that evening, I came to visit patients, and family members, and to do anything else that needed to be done or anything that the nurses needed. In those early years I would work all day and then go in the evening to hospice.

It was a nice calm evening and I had just taken a break after visiting a patient. I sometime take a break in the garden, one of our break rooms or chatting with the nurses at one of our two nurse's stations. It's important to take an emotional break between patient visits!

I walked only one room away from the second story nurse's station and there was a ninety-year-old lady laying quietly in bed. She looked at me and made a small smile. I walked in and introduced myself as a hospice volunteer.

She smiled and nodded at me. I asked her nicely if she would like a visit. She readily agreed for some company. There was a wooden stool by the bed, so I pull it up and gently sat next to her. This lovely ninety-year-old lady had a soft voice so I sat close to her so she would not have to strain her voice.

When I asked her if she was from Houston, Texas, she replied yes, but that she was originally from Philadelphia, Pennsylvania. In order to create a small bond, I replied that I had been to Philadelphia a few times myself. I had been there three times, once just passing through, and twice for work.

She told me that she was born and raised in Philadelphia into a prominent Philadelphia family. Her family was extremely wealthy and well connected in the city and the state.

She was a young seventeen-year-old girl in nineteen-thirty-seven when she meets a young nineteen-year-old

German immigrant. Throughout the nineteen thirties, there was a large migration of German Jews and non-Jews alike leaving Nazi Germany for a safer environment in the United States.

In the summer of nineteen-thirty-seven she fell madly in love with this young handsome German man! Both of them became so happy together! This was the beginning of a love story that would last a lifetime!

Even though they were madly in love with each other, her family was not madly in love with him! They were very wealthy and powerful, and they wanted to become more so. They wanted to marry their daughter off to another wealthy and powerful family in the state to increase their standing in the region.

This love story was the last thing that her family wanted. When he proposed marriage to her, her family intervened and said no to any relationship, and especially no to a marriage! This was not in their plans!

Both of them were devastated about the rejection! But all they could think of was the love that they shared together. They determined that they would stay together no matter what anyone else thought about it. They were in love and that was all that mattered to them!

In order to stay together they had to make a big decision. So, they went to the train station and got on the midnight train going to Chicago, Illinois!

There in Chicago they got married and started their life together! Her husband was a butcher and found work in a local butcher shop and she made a home and started a family.

Her husband had a brother who went to Houston, Texas. After five years in Chicago, they also went to Houston and started their own butcher shop in nearby Bellaire, Texas, close to Houston. In those days there was a small German community in the area.

She then told me that her wealthy family back in Philadelphia never did forgive her and did not reconcile with her. She had been banished! She did not receive any kind of an inheritance from them.

But with a smile on her face from ear to ear, she did not mind. She was always very content to be the wife of the local butcher, her lover, her husband!

As I was talking with her and receiving this beautiful story, she had a radiant glow around her face, and a smile from ear to ear! I had thought that maybe my hair was sticking up during our visit. I had even a few times brushed my hair in order to correct the imagined problem.

I then asked her about her husband. She said with a soft voice that he had died a year ago. She said that she was devastated by his death. But she still had this huge smile! I thought that it was kind of strange she was still smiling!

She then looked at me with loving eye's that were starting to mist over. And she said, "When I arrived here, he met me here!" I asked who met you? She said my husband! He is here now in the room and is waiting for me! I asked her if that was why she was smiling so big. She told me that feeling his presence is a wonderful pleasure and she eager to be in his arms again!

I could not see anyone else in the room, but she could see him. I have never seen a more joyful person then this ninety-year-old lady laying in this bed!

The next week when I returned to the hospice to volunteer, I asked the nursing staff about this lady. I was told that she had passed away a few days previously. Then I knew that the last breath of life that she breathed in, was the first breathe in her lover's arms. They are now spending eternity together!

It was love at first sight

I had been at our hospice for a while visiting with a large family in the downstairs break room. Sometimes like that I kind of feel like an entertainer or a host. Hosting a large family can be a lot of fun, even in an environment like a hospice where family members sometimes need a break from the caring and grieving process, or even to let off some steam.

Afterwards I decided to go upstairs and visit with a patient in one of the rooms. I soon found this older lady lying in bed and alert.

I introduced myself as a volunteer here at the hospice and asked her if she would like some company. She readily agreed. She was in her eighties or nineties, I didn't ask and being a gentleman, I didn't look either.

I sat down next to her and we were having a pleasant conversation together. Her name was Billie, and she was a nice and sharp minded person. It's a blessing to keep your mind sharp until the end.

Eventually I asked Billie how she had met her husband. Then I see this beautiful smile come across her face. Billie said that she met her husband in the military during the war.

Whenever people mention "the war," it is always a reference to World War Two. A lot of people met and fell in love during the war. War brides were very common after the war. Billie and her husband Ben were one of those lucky couples.

Ben was in the U.S. Army and was trained as a B-24 pilot. He was sent to Amarillo Army Air Base, in Amarillo, Texas. Ben was stationed there to be an instructor in B-24 bombers. There his responsibilities would be to train new pilots for the war effort.

After arriving at Amarillo Army Air Base, Ben had to receive a base badge. Ben walked into the base badge office and there sitting behind the desk is our then young Billie. According to our now patient, Billie, they both looked upon each other and fell madly in love with each other!

Billie was also in the U.S. Army as a woman auxiliary officer. Her job was to inspect people's credentials and to issue them base badges for identification. The day that they met was the day that changed both of their lives forever!

Billie stayed at the Amarillo base, but Ben was reassigned to another bomber base in El Paso, Texas. Ben was to be in El Paso for the remainder of the war. Even though they were separated, they stayed in touch by short phone calls and long letters.

Ben told me the next week, when I met him, that the first thing that he did when he heard that the Japanese surrendered was to call Billie in Amarillo and propose marriage! And of course, as I now know, she said yes!

A wonderful wedding

It was a beautiful morning today, warm and dry but a bit breezy. I went to our little volunteer office and found the two bottles of cinnamon that I had left in the following weeks. I can be so absent minded about some things. Whenever I brew a fresh pot of coffee, I always put a bit of cinnamon in the grounds. The cinnamon takes all of the bitterness out of the coffee and gives it a nice smooth taste!

After retrieving my badge, which identifies who I am, I walked into the downstairs break room. Standing next to the coffee pot was a lady in her fifties, with long golden hair.

Armed with a bottle of cinnamon in my hand I walk over to make so coffee. Since this lady is standing nearby, I start to chat with her. "Cindy" was very friendly lady and very easy to talk too. This wonderful lady was the wife of one of our patients.

The lady with the golden hair told me about her upbring in Kansas and how she had met "Donald," her future husband. They eventually came down to Houston to find better employment, which finds them here. Cindy freely told me of all of the medical trials of her Donald's lung cancer that he has been battling for the last few years.

Cindy was also very frustrated and heartbroken over her inability to get her husband on disability. Even though he had a terminal cancer, the disability office had been giving them the runaround. That type of frustration was the last thing that they needed!

When Donald had seen the doctor and had been briefed on the test results, he said that the doctor had informed him that he had four to six years to live. His cancer was terminal and could not be treated!

When his wife met with the doctor, she had found out that he had misunderstood! He really only had four to six months to live! This loving man it seems had tried to protect his wife from the shock of the news!

Once Cindy had found out the real diagnosis, she did not tell him the truth. If he wanted to protect her heart, she would let him!

She now described how they had meet in a store in Kansas where they both lived. They very quickly moved in together. That was thirty years ago! She revealed that because of past unsuccessful love lives for both of them, they decided to just live together.

Because both of them had trust issues the first few years were difficult, but after that the remaining years was wonderful and full of love!

So, last summer when he was diagnosed with lung cancer, they decided to finally get married!

For months afterwards as he endured treatments for his cancer nothing more was said about it. Then a few months ago when Donald met the hospital chaplain, he asked him if he could perform weddings!

Cindy was there and was shocked! But it was a joyful shock! The chaplain replied that he could not perform that ceremony, but he could arrange another that could marry them.

Cindy and Donald had lived together for thirty years, and they had lived quiet and low-keyed lives. They didn't think that anyone would be interested in their wedding, but Cindy sent out invitations by email anyway. With Donald in the hospital Cindy didn't have time for real invitations or the wedding bells and whistles.

To their surprise fifty people showed up at Donald's hospital room for their wedding! They were surprised and overjoyed by all of the support that they were not even aware of. They were happily married, and Cindy gladly took on his name.

Cindy admitted to me that even though they had a wonderful life living together for the last thirty years, it felt different now. They now felt an even closer bond with each other. Cindy said that marriage does make a difference!

She told me now they will spend as much time together and enjoy each other for his last few remaining weeks.

This all reminded me of the cinnamon that I put into the coffee grounds. The cinnamon takes all of the bitterness out of the coffee. That makes the coffee drink nice and smooth. It looked to me that their marriage took a lot of the bitterness out of their situation. That made their relationship with Donald's condition much smoother.

They eloped

It was a beautiful and quiet evening, and I was excited about being at our hospice to be of some service to others. After brewing some coffee at the downstairs break room for our family members, I walked around looking for someone to visit.

I found a room with a ninety-seven-year-old lady! For her age her mind was still very sharp! But she was very hard of hearing, so I had to talk very loudly, which for me is difficult.

I start a conversation with this wonderful lady. She was born and raised in New York City. When she was a young lady in her early twenties, she worked in New York City at a department store called Macy's. Beautiful, but still single, and working full time to support herself showed me that she was an independent lady!

Very often she would go by train from New York City where she lived and go to the Catskill mountains, to go skiing. Sometimes she would go by herself or with some girlfriends. The Catskill mountains are only one-hundred-forty miles directly north of New York City. There are a lot of ski resorts and other recreational activities in the Catskill's. It is commonly called the playground for New Yorkers.

She loved to ski and loved to be with friends of all kinds. She could jump on a train and be in the Catskill's in only three hours. It sounds like a busy and fast passed life, but she was young, outgoing and full of life.

At one of the ski resorts, she met someone! A young German immigrant who had escaped from Nazi Germany and all of the troubles that were happing in Europe. He had a job there and when they met, they fell madly in love with each other!

They started to date and see each other more often. She would go to the Catskill's to ski with him. He would travel to New York City to be with her. They had a fast and very passionate love affair.

When her lover proposed marriage and a lifelong commitment, she said "yes!"

But her family said, "no!'

He was a penniless man from a troubled part of the world. There were concerns about German spies being sent to the United States. Was he a German spy? Germany did have an extensive spy network during the last war! They were just afraid of her brash decision. Why a German immigrant? Was there not plenty of native American men available?

Being the independent folks these two were, they decided to elope and get married without their blessing. A very bold move for her. But her life was full of bold moves!

They took the train for Chicago, Illinois, and got married. This was in the hot summer of nineteen-thirty-eight. They lived in Chicago for the next three years, until he got a job in Houston, Texas. He worked for Continental Airlines as an economic strategist. They lived in Houston for the rest of their lives.

He lived to be an old man and passed away. A couple years later, she has only a few days left, and I am blessed to talk with her and to bear witness to her love story. I leaned over and told her that her husband was a smart man. She answered, "yes he was, he married me!" With that answer we both laughed! What a great lady!

In today's world that seems like the norm. Women today are enjoying those freedoms and much more. But, here, we are talking about the nineteen-thirties! Women's lives in those days were much more restricted than they are today. That is what make her story much more fascinating!

He whistled at her

I was in a patient's room speaking with a middle-aged lady and her mother. Her mother was the patient and was lying in bed. Her mother is ninety-six-years-old! Her father is ninety-eight-years-old!

Her mother and her family had escaped from Nazi Germany during the Second-World War! Her mother and her family were Germans, but her father was an accountant, and he was helping Jewish families who were trying to flee the country. He was sending money overseas as the Jewish families attempted to sneak out of Germany.

When the German Gestapo was getting close, the son was secretly sent to England and the daughter, our patient, was secretly sent to live with an Aunt in Prague, Czechoslovakia. She lived there for two years until she could find a safe passage out of German controlled territory. She did eventually make it safe to England, and rejoined her brother, who had already established himself there.

She was an eighteen-year-old lady by that time and had secured a job in England. One day she was walking in

27

a local park, around noon, when she heard a whistle! She quickly looked behind her and immediately spotted an American serviceman. He was looking at her and was smiling! Yup, he was the one who had whistled at her! She slowly turned around, looking at him up and down with approval.

She slowly walked up to him and said, "Today is my eighteenth birthday, are you going to take me out to lunch?" He did take her out to lunch that day, and many days after that, until they were married!

That one whistled started a beautiful romance that lasted for over sixty years! When the war was over, they both moved to Texas and lived, and raised a family together. That just goes to show you what one whistle can start! All it can take to change your life forever is just one little whistle!

He had been her whole life!

I was at the hospice with a shadow today. A "shadow" is a new volunteer who is tagging along a seasoned volunteer. She was a very nice middle-aged lady and was doing a great job!

We had walked into a room with an elderly man, in his late nineties, lying in bed and three middle-aged ladies with him. Those three ladies were his granddaughters.

They were very attractive and very friendly. As soon as we walked into the room and introduced ourselves, they just immediately included us in their family meeting.

They were about their grandfather's bed as he peacefully rested. The ladies were very concerned about their grandfather's care.

He was resting quietly now, but they said that last night, he was very restless. It was very obvious to me that they loved their grandfather very much! This man was very blessed!

They shared with my shadow and I in glowing voices that their grandparents had been married for seventy-one years!

Their grandmother was still alive, she was also in her nineties. She was in deep mourning they said! She was married to him for seventy-one years and didn't know what she was going to do without him!

The granddaughters shared with us how their grandmother had taken such good care of her husband when he became sick. She cooked great home cooked meals and took loving care of him. She would always say, "he has been my whole life!

Their grandmother was not here yet, but she was coming here soon. They had a big family and was concerned about letting too many people into the room. They were a big Irish American Catholic family and there was a lot of love in the room. I think that this man had been everyone's whole life!

I was the lucky one!

I was at the hospice on a beautiful Saturday morning. I had a shadow with me today. A shadow is a new hospice volunteer who is following along with an experienced volunteer.

My shadow today is a young twenty-one-year-old Hispanic lady. She plans on going on to medical school and become a future doctor! Being expose to hospice care will be a great asset to her in the future.

My shadow and I were walking around to different rooms and were having a good day. Then we walked into a room with an older Englishman lying in bed, who was originally from Newcastle, England.

He had worked in the oil business all of his life, and he was an expert in pumps and compressors. Oil fields and refineries are all about pumps and compressors!

After a lifetime in the oil business and traveling all over the world, literally, all over the world, his last stop was in Humble, Texas. They were here in Texas a long time and so decided to retire here as well.

He was married as a young man to his bride. They eventually had two daughters together. The first daughter was born in England and the second one was born in Texas.

They traveled all over the world together as a family. Everywhere in the world he went, his loving wife and family followed him.

I noticed that he had a picture of a lady on the table next to him. I asked him if that was his wife. He said that she was and that she had passed away a few years ago.

I took the picture off of the table and looked at it. I told him that she was a beautiful lady! I then showed it to my shadow, who had been quietly sitting next to me.

I then asked him how they had met each other. He said that they had met at a dance, and he had fell in love with her at first sight!

He said that they fell in love with each other and quickly got married! When he started to work in the oil business, she followed him all over the world with him!

I told him that she was a lucky woman to be married to him. He looked at me and pointed at his chest and said, "I was the lucky one!"

A tear came to his eyes, and he repeated himself, "I was the lucky one!" I told him that I think that they were both very lucky to have each other. They were both the lucky ones!

He was choked up and could not speak. A tear slowly came down his chiseled face, as he held tightly to his wife's picture. I told him that he will see her again. He looked at me and just nodded, "yes!"

Ghost Stories

My ghost story

It was a nice spring Saturday around noon sometime. I had a shadow for the last three hours. A shadow is a new hospice volunteer who is tagging along with an experienced volunteer to learn the ropes.

We had been visiting several patients and family members and have a nice time. My shadow was an elderly lady in her sixties and was doing a wonderful job. The last patient I didn't even have to do anything, she did everything!

We had finished and were hanging out at the second-floor nurses' station, just taking a break. I looked down the hallway, about thirty feet, and viewed an adult man.

The adult man walked from the left corner of the room to the right side of the room where the bed is located. The two rooms at the end of the hallway are larger than the other rooms. I clearly saw the man and didn't think too much of it.

So, I glance to my right and wave my hand and say to my shadow, "there is someone we can visit." We immediately start to walk over to the room. With my long legs, it doesn't take long to travel thirty feet. As I was walking to the room, I was looking for signs of other people or things inside.

As we got to the doorway, my shadow dropped behind me and said, "I'll let you go first!" I don't think that she seen the man, she was just a new volunteer and was a bit timid still.

I walk in expecting to see a man sitting on the couch by the bed and a patient in the bed. Since I had seen a man, I boldly walk in to introduce myself. If I had seen a woman, I would have walked in more slowly, because women get startled much easily.

I walk in and there is nobody in the room! The bed to the right is even empty! No patient and no other people in the room! I look in the bathroom, nobody! If anyone had walked out of the room, I would have seen them. I clearly saw a man walk from left to right inside the room!

Because I have a brand-new hospice volunteer at my side, I needed to keep my cool. I told her that I had clearly seen a man in the room, but I didn't act panicky for her sake. I didn't want to scare her off and have her quit.

So, I told her that that was strange, I had seen someone, but now he is gone. I certainly didn't tell her that that room and the next room is famous for ghost children being reported there.

I was in the next room years ago, visiting a patient, when the patient saw two children behind me. Children that I could not see myself! There were many other reports of ghost children in these two rooms. But I had seen an adult man, not a child. I don't know, maybe he was there to collect the children and to take them home!

Men with clipboards

On one fine Saturday morning I was visiting with a man in his sixties. He was a patient, and alert and watching television. He was college educated professional and had been very successful in life.

I was with him for about thirty minutes as he ate lunch and watched television. I just made myself fit into his rhythm of life here at our hospice.

We were talking about a lot of different subjects. Then he turned towards me with a serous face. He said that he had been seeing visitations. A visitation is when a dying patient see things, or other people, that no one else can see! This is a common accordance within two weeks before death.

He had seen an elevator with two men using it to go to both floors. These men were dressed in suit and ties and had clipboards in their hands. He said that these men were moving from room to room walking through the halls and checking on all of the patients and looking and writing on their clipboards!

With a serous voice, he told me that he had been seeing the same two men every evening! He was not frightened by the visitations, but instead, fascinated by them!

I didn't tell him that seeing visitations was a sign of just a few weeks to live, but I'm sure the doctors did tell him. I just told him that the sighting was amazing and that he should take it as a blessing!

I have always thought afterwards, if maybe, those two men with their clipboards, paid him a visit, when it was his time to pass to the other side!

The white-haired boy and a baby

It was a Friday afternoon and a very busy day at our hospice. When I arrived for service, the nurses immediately told me about a very nice lady who would enjoy some company.

She was upstairs, now the second floor, it was the top floor back then. I walk down the hallway to room two-seventeen. It is all the way in the back and around a small corner.

As I entered the room, I see a middle-aged Hispanic lady in bed. I introduced myself as a volunteer and ask if she would like some company. She readily agrees, and she mentioned that other volunteers had already been there. It seems that she cannot get enough visits. I soon found out why, she is quit the talker!

She is a little lady and a bit plump! Being of a normal weight or a bit over normal is a rare condition at a hospice. I didn't look to see what her condition was, I never do, since it is not my business to know. It's usually a good sign!

She was very alert and clear minded and spoke very well. Something else unusual in hospice care. She looked like she could just walk out of there any time she wanted. That all made for a more relaxed and a nicer visit.

She began to tell me about her upbringing in Central Texas countryside on a farm. Her family grew cotton, raised chickens and pigs. This was a normal lifestyle for a farm family in Texas.

She talked about school, church, and weekly town dances. The town dances took place at the town school or a large barn near the town. She said that they all loved to dance and socialize on those warm Saturday nights!

I eagerly listened as she talked about her past and the nursing home in Austin, Texas, where she was going. She had a daughter in Austin, which is why she is going there.

We talked for over four hours together! We had such a nice visit that the time just flew by! At that point, her son and granddaughter came into the room. As is my custom, I stood up to excuse myself, since family has arrived. The son looked like he was in his late twenties and his daughter was about ten years old. Both were wonderful folks.

I tried to excuse myself, but both of them literally begged me to stay with them! I humbly agreed to stay and tried to stay out of the way. The four of us sat and had a very pleasant visit. The son was very friendly, but his daughter seemed to be very nervous and uncomfortable. That is a common emotion in that type of an environment. They stayed and visited for about thirty minutes.

When they left, I was again alone with her, but it was about time for me to leave as well. But I wanted to be polite, so I decided to stay a little longer. I'm glad that I did because things started to get much more interesting!

We chatted again for about thirty minutes when I noticed that she was looking at the other side of the room behind me with a very concerned look and a more serious continence upon her face! It was hard for me not to notice it and I asked her what was the problem?

She peered over my shoulder and asked me who was that boy sitting there next to the wall! I looked around and behind me and I didn't see anyone else in the room!

A little startled, I asked her, "what boy?" She replied, "the white-haired boy sitting by the baby!" I again looked behind me and I didn't see anyone. But she for certain was seeing them! She was getting more tense and nervous!

She was seeing a white-haired boy and a baby that I could not see! I kept my cool so that she would not become fearful. That room and the one next to it have a reputation of people seeing children in them!

I was with her for a little over five hours already and I was needing to leave and call it a day. I didn't want her to be fearful when I left, so I told her that the white-haired boy and the baby were family members who have come to visit with her.

When I told her that she immediately calmed down and relaxed. That made all of the difference. She loves to visit! Instead of two strange and spooky people, they were now visitors!

When I was assured that she was to be alright, I excused myself and called it a day, and what a day it was! I later was informed that she had been moved to Austin, Texas, where she passed away two weeks later!

When I told others in the hospice about the sighting, no one was surprised. I found out that it is a common occurrence for patients in the last few weeks of life to see other people that had passed away years before, or others that people cannot see!

I learned that day that we are truly not alone, and that when it is our time to pass on, that someone, a loved one or someone else, will be there for us to ease the transition!

The blue people

I had just visited with a patient and came out of the room. I walked over to the nurse's station and took a small break with them. When I arrived, they were in the middle of a conversation.

They were kind of in an amazement about a series of sightings by several of the patients today. The nurses were confirming with each other that several of the patients that day had reported seeing blue people!

Several of the patients had seen blue people walking around and even talking with some of the patients. They had said that they looked kind of like the blue people from the play that was playing years ago called, "Blue people."

These hospice nurses have been around awhile and have heard many stories of blue people being reported by the patients in the past. Those sightings are usually very rare they said. They would hear about it only once in a while.

What was different about today, and which caught the attention of the nurses on duty, was the number of sightings today. Normally those sighting were constant, but rare. Just today they had already had several sightings, that was what made it different and got the attention of the nursing staff!

I have heard of a lot a strange thing in my years as a hospice volunteer, but this was an odd one indeed. Most things we can kind of explain, even a little bit. But this one is unexplainable. But we only know of this world? We know nothing of the worlds in existence, or even the world to come!

Too many patients see things!

I was at our hospice on a Saturday afternoon, standing at the nurse's station. I was in-between patient visits and taking a little break. Three nurses and I were talking about hospice care and the people we deal with on a daily basis.

At first, they were talking about some difficult family members. There is usually no shortage of those folks. Then the conversation turned into patient testimonies of them seeing things.

One of our long-term nurse's didn't believe in the sightings that people would see in our building. The other two nurse's and I as well, admitted that we all had been with patients that were seeing people in the spirit world.

The nurse who didn't believe it, even she had been with patient's that had seen something! She finally joined us in admitting that a lot of patients had seen loved ones that had passed away previously.

Some patients see loved ones who passed away already, they sometimes see strangers that they don't know, and some rare occasions they have even seen blue people. These were all sightings that only the patient could see, and no one else!

We all took turns and told our stories of being with patients who were seeing things or people. A lot of times they have seen children running around.

In the end we all agreed that there is a physical world that we are all currently living in, and there is a spiritual world that is unseen. A few days to a few weeks, patients are able to see beyond the veil of death and see what is beyond it temporarily.

We could not explain it, but we are all witnesses that it does indeed happen. Even people who are not dying can sometimes see ghosts in the building. I have seen a middle-aged man in a room, only to find out that the room was empty. Others have seen a young girl playing by the back door.

No matter what your belief system is, there is a life beyond the veil of death. Death is not an ending, but instead, just a new beginning in a different world or existence. The folks who work in the hospice industry have all heard the stories and the testimonies of the patients. When our soul departs this body, it goes somewhere, somewhere out there! Nobody really dies alone; we are headed someplace very crowded!

The girl by the door

I was at our hospice on a Saturday morning standing at the second-floor nurse's station. I often take a small break there in between patient visits. It's always good to refocus for a few minutes.

When I walked up to the counter, the nurses were already having a conversation about some strange things that happen around the campus!

They had just been talking about the ghost children that are often seen or heard at the two rooms at the end of the hallway.

Then "Ann", the Charge Nurse and another volunteer hanging out with us then brought up the sightings by the girl near the back door!

I knew exactly what they were talking about. By the back door, on the ground floor, leading out to the back garden, we have had many sightings!

The girl, of about ten-years-old, plays just inside and just outside the back door. By the back door is the chapel and the old mansion and that opens up to the back garden.

Some of the nurses who have seen her at night, have tried to speak with her, but she will just vanish away. She has been seen by different people at different times.

Everyone who has seen her, have said that it was always a friendly and positive sighting. The girl was always nice and didn't seem to be in any type of distress or anything.

I have not personally seen this girl, but a patient that I had rolled out in that area did see a little boy that I could not see myself. This little boy has been seen not just there but all over the campus.

The girl just plays around in that area for some unknown reason. Ghosts don't have to be scary! Sometimes it can be a positive experience!

Ice cream with his brothers

    I was at our hospice for a few hours by the time I had this visit. I had a shadow with me all day. She was a middle-ages lady and she was very fun to hang out with. A shadow is a brand-new volunteer that is tagging along with an experienced volunteer for some on-the-job-training.

    We now walked in a room with a ninety-five-year-old patient lying in bed. He was the brother of the mayor of our large city. He had two other brothers as well. For privacy reasons I do not want to name the city, our hospice, or the people involved.

    When we walked in, he was lying in bed, and he had three pretty middle-aged granddaughters with him. We stood there and chatted for a while. I was a little surprised because they were so friendly! Their family was one of the richest families in the city, if not the State. For being so wealthy, they were very friendly and inclusive.

    While we were talking, they shared a great story with my shadow and I. The three granddaughters came to the hospice early in the morning, their granddad was already awake.

He had told his granddaughters that he was awake long before breakfast in the quiet early morning hours as dawn was just peeking over the horizon.

Then he said that his three brothers walked into the room! They had with them cartoons of ice cream. They said that it was time for an ice cream party! So, they all sat down and eat ice cream together and swapped stories about growing up together.

They all brought ice cream for everyone except one of them. That was the brother who had been the mayor. It was an inside family joke! But they all shared with him and they all had a good laugh and had a great time together.

The granddaughters, very astonished by now, asked their grandfather if they were really his brothers or not. He said, of course they were, I may be old and dying, but I know my brothers when I see them!

But granddad, they exclaimed, all of your brothers have been dead for years now!

War Stories

Vietnam or Jail

I was sitting with an elderly man while he quietly rested in his bed. I was there because his nurse shared with me that when he wakes up alone, he becomes frightened, as a result of his medication he was receiving to deal with his medical condition.

While I was there by the bedside, just being there for the patient, his wife walks in quickly. She had come in a huff because she had left her phone in the room last night. She was with her husband until three in the morning! She was so tired when she left for the night, she had forgotten her phone in the room. That's a big deal for almost everyone these days!

I had seen the phone on the bedside table when I had come in be with her husband. When she came in, she explained very quickly if her phone was in the room. I smiled at her and pointed to the table, her phone clearly laying on it.

She was openly relieved! This elderly lady has had a lot going on lately, none of it good, and replacing her phone was the last time that she needed. After I introduced myself as a hospice volunteer, she thanked me for being there and keeping her phone safe! I told her that it was my pleasure.

She sat down and insisted that I stay. I readily agreed, since it appeared that she needed someone to talk to. My discernment was correct. I soon found out that this lady was dealing with a lot of stress and grief over her husband's condition!

After consoling her for a while, she told me that she worked for a local Christian High School raising money for remodeling. She had already raised thirty-million dollars of a goal of raising eighty-million dollars for the school remodel. I was immediately impressed with her position and success in her carrier.

53

She then confided in me that a lot of her wealthy donors were also donors to our hospice, which is a non-profit hospice. We both went to Catholic schools, and we swapped stories about the nuns who ran them! We also went through flight training to become pilots. So, we had a lot of stories about flying. We had a lot in common and were enjoying ourselves.

Then we started to talk about her loving husband. She told me that he had received a draft notice to go into the U.S. Army. Well, he didn't want to go to war! So, he refused to report to the Army! The Viet Nam war was going on and folks were getting killed there.

Not showing up when drafted is against the law, so the police came around and picked him up and transported him to jail. The judge now told him that he had to do two tours in Viet Nam instead of just one, or he had to spend that amount or longer in prison! He chose the Army over jail!

The Army trained him to be part of a special security unit that would be behind enemy lines and to rescue American servicemen who were in trouble. They operated in small units and would spend weeks to months behind enemy lines. She told me that he spent many days and nights surrounded by enemy soldiers!

It was such a dangerous duty, and being so close to the enemy, they most of the time dared not sleep! If you fell asleep so close to the enemy you may not wake up! When his unit would finally return to their base, they would be totally exhausted!

One day after a long deployment behind enemy lines, he fell asleep outside. He went to sleep along the road on the American Military Base at Da Nang. He went to sleep there because he felt safe hearing the noise of fellow American troops. If he went to bed in a quiet barracks and heard a sudden noise, he would freak out, thinking it would be the enemy!

One day a Colonel had seen him there along the road asleep and had him arrested! When a General, who had known who he was and where he had come out of, very quickly gave the Colonel a "dressing down!" She told me that that General told her husband that he could sleep anywhere he wanted! The General understood!

I told her that her husband was a very brave man! I told her that my own father was stationed at Da Nang. He was a medic, and the two men might have crossed paths there in Viet Nam! And now here we are, talking about both of them!

Her husband returned from Viet Nam; his duty done! He worked professionally as a bass player. He played with Mickey Gilley and other famous singers and bands. Thousands of people would see him up on the stage in the background and no one would know him, or what he had been through for two years! As he played entertainment for others, there were two years of hell in his mind that was kept secret!

The B-17 gunner

I had a very nice visit with an elderly man on a Saturday afternoon. We spent an hour and a half talking about his upbringing on a farm in the Spring Branch area. That was very interesting to me because that whole area is now part of the city of Houston. Thousands of people drive those roads every day have no idea what had been there in the past!

After I asked him, he then mentioned that he served in Second World War. He was very modest about his service and didn't make a big deal about it. I always think that military service during war years is always a big deal!

This mild-mannered gentleman before me was a B-17 tail gunner! He was stationed with a bomber group in Italy. They flew mission into the Balkans, which was under German control at the time. They also were able to fly bomber missions into Southern Germany, and German occupied Eastern Europe.

He said that he flew in twenty-five missions over Germany proper of German controlled Europe. That was the number of missions that bomber crews had to fly to be discharged and sent home. Many crews never made it home!

I asked him what he remembers most about his service as a bomber tail gunner. He said something that I didn't expect, He said, "the cold!" He admitted that the extreme cold is what he most remembers.

When the bombed targets in Germany, they had to fly high over the Alps! The Alps are very high and they had to fly even higher to get over them. The temperature at those heights could get to fifty degrees below zero!

They had to just bundle up and endure it as they were also on oxygen. There is no oxygen at those heights! So, survival over the elements was the first goal even before they could get to Germany!

Once they crossed the Alps, the German fighters would be waiting for them. The temperature would still be very cold, but with their oxygen masks on, they had to fight them off! After the fighters had their chance then the anti-aircraft guns would start shooting at them!

The surviving bombers would then attack the target. Once that was done, they had to endure everything all over again to get back to their base in Italy! They all had to do that twenty-five times before they could go back home!

Seventy-five percent would not make that twenty-five-mission number! They would die in the air, die on the ground after getting shot down, or captured behind enemy lines!

The man lying in his bed in front of me did survive! He did make his twenty-five-missions! When the call for duty rang out, he stood up and showed up! Then he returned home and made a good life for himself.

Pearl Harbor survivor

I walked into a room to visit with the folks inside. There was an elderly lady who was the patient lying in bed unconscious. Her husband, who we will call "Jack," was there sitting with her and taking care of her needs. He showed a lot of love and compassion for his dying wife. Jack was a very nice, and talkative ninety-year-old man.

When I said that he is a talker, I mean he talked for three hours non-stop! Then when his brother showed up, he talked even longer! But he was a very interesting man and it was a joy to listen to him!

Jack was not just a nice elderly man; he was a Pearl Harbor survivor! Very few people can say that now. Most of the men at Pearl Harbor on December seventh, nineteen forty-one, are now passed away. So, it was quite an honor for me to meet one of the few surviving ones!

During the Pearl Harbor attack by planes of the Japanese Imperial Navy, Jack was below decks on the Battleship Nevada. He was below decks on this quiet Sunday morning playing poker with several other crewmen.

They were sitting at the "poker table" all in their standard white navy underwear! That's because in nineteen-forty-one, there was no air conditioning! Not only that, but they were serving on an all-metal battleship that would absorb the heat.

So, because of no air conditioning it was common for the guys that were off duty to stay in their underwear all day. Playing poker for pennies was a very common game back then, since pennies was all that young navy guys could afford!

During the start of the attack, they heard the planes coming, but the guys just thought that the U.S. Navy planes were flying that Sunday morning. They were sitting in a large Navy base after all, so they just kept playing poker.

When the bombs started to explode, the "battle stations" sirens went off! Confused about the explosions and sirens, they ran up the stairs. When they got topside, they saw the planes flying overhead with big red balls on their wings!

That meant that instead of American planes as they thought, they were Japanese Navy planes! When they saw the planes, that they then knew exactly what was going on. They were at war!

Jack said that everyone ran to their battle stations. He was near the edge of the ship at the same time that a Japanese torpedo stuck the ship and exploded! He was thrown up and away from the ship and landed in the water. The explosion actually saved his life since it blew him clear of the ship! As the battle continued, he watched it surrounded by burning oil and gasoline!

As he was floating in the water, his ship, the Battleship Nevada, started to sail away. Its captain intended to take his ship out of the harbor and into open water. They didn't make it, after taking on more battle damage, the

60

captain ordered his ship to ground on a sand bar so it would not sink in the channel!

Jack then swam to the shore and was safe and sound! He said that after the battle, he was reassigned to other ships in the war and had seen every major battle of the war. His brother also served in the Navy, but he only worked a typewriter for the entire war.

Jack then told me a story that he had kept secret for all of his life. He said that when his ship was in Alaska, he got to go on shore leave, and got very drunk. Being drunk, he got into a fistfight with someone and was arrested by Navy shore patrol. He was always embarrassed by that incident!

Just after he shared that story with me, his ninety-two-year-old brother walks into the room. Both of these gentlemen were in their nineties, but they were in excellent health and could walk around as well as anyone. His brother is also very friendly and talkative.

As we visited, his brother told us a story about his Navy service. He also had shore leave one day and also got drunk and got into a fistfight! He also was arrested by Navy shore patrol! It was almost the identical story! His brother also had kept it a secret from his family all of these years!

Jack smiled and looked at his brother in total amazement! Jack told him about the tale he had just shared with me, almost the same story! Both of these men had the same incident in the Navy, and both had kept it a secret until now!

The three of us just laughed and had a wonderful moment together! Both of these men relieved themselves of their past. It was certainly a special moment for me, since I was the third party who was the catalyst for this special moment of sharing!

The switchboard operator

It was a beautiful Saturday morning, and I was being shadowed by a new trainee. A large, muscular and fit African American man in his late forties. He had just retired from the U.S Army. He is now in school to be a counselor. He has a good heart and wants to make a difference in the world. I'm sure that when he is ready, the Lord will bless the work of his hands.

When we walked down the hall to the downstairs nurse's station, we were meet by one of the nurses. I could tell by the look on her face that she had a request. As we arrived, she had a smile on her face.

She had a patient's room with a broken pull-out couch. Each of our rooms have a small couch that pulls out into a bed. Many family members want to stay with their loved ones. So, much of our furniture doubles as beds. We also have showers and washing machines available on-site, and also have a full kitchen.

With a smile on our faces, we both readily agreed to help her out. It is Saturday and the maintenance man needs to take a few days off. I am not the handiest of men, but I was soon to find out that my shadow is indeed.

We eagerly walk into the room. The room was directly across the hallway from the nurse's station. The patient was an elderly French lady. Her two daughters were also there. One daughter was talking to the doctor in another room, and the other one was in the room with her mother.

A third lady was sitting on a wooden stool next to the patient. She was a granddaughter, and we were to find out that she doubled as an interpreter. The two daughters could speak French, but the granddaughter was still learning and was enjoying the responsibility.

The patient needed an interpreter because she could not speak any English! Both her and her American husband had lived in France most of their lives and had come her for medical treatment.

The granddaughter was a young lady who lives in Brooklyn, New York. She is going to college there and flew down here to be with her grandmother in her last days. She is a very sweet young lady.

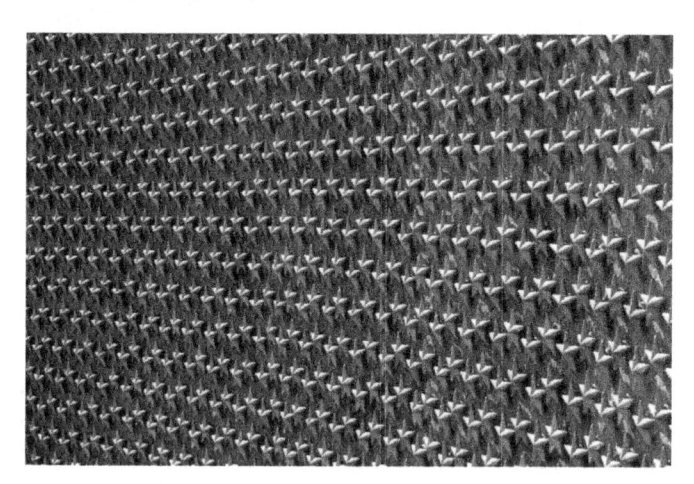

My shadow and I check out the couch. We soon discover that the wheels inside were off of their track on one side. We pulled on the frame and got it back on track. I have to confess that my large, muscular shadow did most of it. With that done, everyone was now happy.

With that chore done, the daughter stands up and thanks us for helping them. I see that as a good opportunity to start up a conversation. I am always looking for a conversation!

The daughter shares with us that her mother was a switchboard operator in French controlled North Africa, before and during the Second World War. When the American Army landed in North Africa in nineteen-forty-two, she started to work for the Americans.

She was a French patriot and was eager to work for the Americans to help liberate her country from the German occupiers! She worked for the American Army as a switchboard operator and as a French interpreter.

When she started working for the American Army in North Africa, she was only sixteen years old! A young lady having to make big decisions! It was there that she met her future husband, an American in General George Patton's Army.

As the war went on into France, Italy, and then Germany, our mother went with it. Working as a switchboard operator and a French interpreter. She was still only seventeen-years-old! Our mom and dad kept in touch by letters. When the war was finally over, they both went to France where they married and lived for all of these years!

Our mother was a living testimonial that women were also part of the war movement. In the years of war and chaos, our mom and dad found each other and fell in love. In the years of cancer, they were now separated, but will now put them back into their arms again!

The escape

I came into our hospice on a Thursday morning. I was off from work that day so I took advantage of the free time to assist others in their time of need. I was grateful that I did because I meet a very interesting elderly gentleman!

I walked into a room with the man lying in bed. The nurse had just left after picking up the breakfast plates after he had eaten. I walked in and introduced myself as a hospice volunteer and asked him if he would like someone to visit with him. He was very friendly and readily agreed.

I found out that he was ninety-eight-year-old man! For his age he looked great, and his mind was still very sharp, I was impressed! I told him that I wish that I would look so good at his age!

I asked him where he was from, thinking that he was a local guy, I was sure wrong! He then started to tell me his life story. And what a great story it was indeed!

He was a Jewish-German man who had immigrated to the United States in nineteen-thirty-seven. His family in Germany was under intense pressure from the Nazi regime. Some of the German-Jewish population was disappearing, their windows were being broken, their shops and homes

67

were being vandalized! Some were being murdered in the streets! Many Jews were trying to get out of Germany, some were determined to stay.

This man's family got together and agreed upon a plan of escape. This man was born in Germany in Nineteen-fifteen and was twenty-two-years-old at the time. The plan was for him to immigrate to New York City, in the United States. Then he could send for the rest of the family.

That was a huge amount of responsibility for a young man. In order to save his entire family, he had to succeed! He successfully immigrated to New York City. The first thing that he had to do was to find a job, being a young man, it was easier than most, and he found one. Then, he worked on the immigration process for his family. Then he saved enough money to secure a large enough place for his family to live while they in turn put down roots.

He was a hard worker and eventually got his entire family here to the United States before the war closed off immigration routes! He did it! He got his entire family to safety from the Nazis!

Once his entire family was safe, he made the decision in the early months of nineteen-forty-one to give back to the United States. He decided to join the American Army. The war in Europe had by this time begun, but the United States was still not involved. It was months before the attack on Pearl Harbor, and we were still at peace.

But, by this time, this man who was twenty-five years old by this time wanted to give back to the nation that provided safety to his family who were now safe. The only way he thought that he could was in the service of the growing American Army.

When the Army found out that he was from Germany and spoke fluent German, they made him a German interpreter. Even though the United States was not at war with Germany, they suspected that they should get ready for one! German speaking interpreters would be in great need if involvement in the raging war would drag us into it. He served as a German interpreter until the end of the war in Europe.

Just before the end of the conflict, he was wounded by shrapnel from a bomb blast in Belgium. He was sent to a hospital in now occupied Germany, then in England, then back to America.

While he was recuperating in occupied Germany, he had the opportunity to visit his old home village, and to visit with the people. Even though the conditions were unpleasant when he left, the visit with his old hometown was positive.

With the war over, and his Army service over, and some metals dangling from his chest, he returned home to New York City. He eventually moved down to Laredo, Texas, and then to Houston, Texas, where he is now.

This man had lived more life before he was twenty-five then we do in a lifetime! His life is what Hollywood movies are made of! This man was grateful for this country and served it well. He didn't just stand around and wait to be drafted, he enlisted before everyone else, and served for the entire duration of the war. He is what heroes are made of!

10ᵗʰ mountain division

I had just walked around the hospice looking for a couple of bowls for a young lady in her thirties. She had brought her two dogs here to visit her mother, who was a patient. She had forgotten her dog bowls, and she needed to feed her dogs.

I had found two bowls, a big one and a small one. She had a big dog and a little dog. I got the bowls and was returning. I pass the break room and rounded the corner to go down the first-floor hallway, their room was the third on the right.

But as I rounded the corner, she was right there standing with an elderly man. I greet the young lady and give her the dog bowls. She takes them and smiles and thanks me.

The three of us are standing there and I see a pin on the older gentleman's shirt. It had a number ten on the pin. I asked the man what the pin meant. When I said that, the man lightened up and stood a bit straighter.

I glance at the young lady, which I find out is his daughter. She rolled her eyes and started walking down the hallway to her mother's room! Sounds like a story was coming that she had heard a million times already. She was right!

With a smile on his face, the older gentleman puts his fingers on the army pin. He said that his father had been in the Tenth Mountain Division in the Second World War in Italy!

He described how the division was formed to fight the enemy in difficult mountain conditions. He even mentioned that they had made a documentary film about the division and what they had accomplished.

The Tenth Mountain Division was the last unit to be formed and the last to be pulled from action. That unit did some impossible tasks against, and behind enemy lines.

He then shared with me how his father had stepped on a land mine, which blew him into another land mine, which then blew him into a third land mine!

The first land mine had killed him, but it seems that the other two land mine he destroyed saved other soldiers! When he described his father's death, I could see the pain and hurt in his voice and all over his face!

He then shared with me that he was too young to remember his father. He was only a baby at the time. He said that he would give anything to have known his father. If only he could just talk with him, if only for a few minutes! I gently touched his arm and I said that soon he will see him, and he would have all eternity to talk with him!

He readily agreed! He said that until then, he was going to wear his father's army pin, and talk about his service and sacrifice to our country. By doing that he can keep his memory alive and keep his father close to his heart!

That story, and the man, really touched me! When I left the hospice for the day, I went home and looked up that documentary film about his father's unit. I watched it in amazement at what they had done during the war!

After the film was over, I solemnly looked up and told his father, thank you for your service and sacrifice. I told him that his son loves him and is keeping his memory alive!

A sickness that saved him

I was sitting with an older lady named "Wilhelmina." She was a very nice Czech American lady in her nineties. Wilhelmina had cancer in her upper back around her spine. Because of that location, it was difficult for her to be comfortable lying-in bed.

Wilhelmina was a nice lady, but totally the quiet type. Her son was sitting next to me on the couch, and he was the opposite of her, he was the talkative type.

Her son's name was "Thomas," and he was in his late sixties or maybe even seventy. He had a big belly, white shirt and black pants and wearing sandals.

I thought that it was kind of odd that he was wearing sandals. He just wasn't the type to wear sandals. I suspected that he had some problem with his feet. I didn't ask, since that would have been rude. I thought that he would have mentioned it himself, but he never did.

Thomas also had thin gray hair and a big smile. I would also soon discover that he had a healthy fixation on the old family farm in Shiner, Texas, where he had grown up. But I'll talk about that at a different time. This story is about his late father, "Larry," and the husband of the patient.

His father was drafted into the United States Army during the Korean War. He was sent to Fort Sill in Oklahoma to be trained in artillery. He finished his training and was now an artilleryman.

When the training was complete, the entire unit was transported by train to San Francisco, California, to take a ship to Korea. From there their future would be unknown!

While they were all waiting around for their ship to arrive to take them all to Korea, Larry came down with a contagious illness! When the doctors diagnosed him, Larry was sent to the base hospital.

While Larry was still in the hospital and still sick, the ship arrived. Larry's unit was loaded up with their guns and they left for the Korean War.

When Larry got healthy again, they decided to reassign him to another unit. They returned him back to Fort Sill in Oklahoma and be a part of the first surface to surface missile program!

Because Larry was no longer going to Korea and was back at Fort Sill, Wilhelmina, now his new bride, was able to join him there. Both of them were of Czech origin and both grew up in the Shiner, Texas area. They had met and married just before he was drafted into the Army.

They were in the Army for four years, when Larry was discharged. They returned to the family farm, and then to Houston, Texas. There they lived a blessed life together.

Larry in later years developed skin cancer twice and was cured. When he got it a third time, the cancer overcame him. Now, his wife has a cancer which will overcome her. Soon, they will be together again! But they always remembered, a long time ago, the time that a sickness that had saved him!

Spiritual Stories

The prayer

    I started this quiet Saturday evening with a very nice elderly lady who is to be discharged on Monday. She has family in Austin, Texas, and will be with her family who will take care of her for the few months that she has to live. We visited for about thirty minutes until she received a phone call, I quickly excused myself.

    I went to another room and saw a group of African American folks inside. The patient and a daughter and eight members of their church prayer group were in the room! We had a wonderful time talking about the Bible, and God's Will and Ways, and the power of the Holy Spirit.

    We visited for about an hour and had great Christian fellowship. It is always a joy to fellowship with fellow Christians. Only fellow Christians can understand the ways of the Holy Spirit and how the Lord works through people and His Word.

Well, at the end of our meeting, when I had to leave for the evening, they asked me to lead them in prayer! We all held hands together around the patient, whom was in bed. I gave a good prayer for strength and direction. Everyone was overjoyed with the prayer, probably because I was new to the group.

After my prayer was completed, the whole group broke out into a Holy Spirit worship! When I was going out of the room, the leader of the prayer group called me their angel! I could feel the Presence of the Lord in a very strong way! They were a great prayer group! We had a wonderful move of God that evening!

Having your family with you in your last days is a blessing. Having your church family with you, and praying with you, and worshiping with you is an even greater blessing!

Some Bible reading

It was a nice quiet evening at the hospice. I went to the break room, made some coffee and put out some cookies out on a plate. Just because everybody needs a snack sometimes.

After that I make my way down the hallway. We had a lot of family members visiting here this evening. That is always a good thing to see. I am here to visit folks, but everyone would rather have their family around, instead of me!

One of the nurses told me of a man in one of the rooms that I could sit with. As I walked into the room, I view the scene. An elderly African-American man was lying unconscious in bed. A small table was next to him with a Bible on it. Otherwise, the room was bare.

I quietly walk around the bed. I softly introduce myself to the gentleman. Even though he is unconscious, he probably could hear me. The sense of hearing is the last of the senses to go. The respectful thing to do is to announce my presence and why I am there.

I gently pick up the Bible laying on the table. It has his name on it, and handwritten notes in it. It is obviously his personnel Bible! I decide that instead of quietly sitting with him, I would read his Bible to him!

I start reading about the birth of Jesus Christ. He is the Prince of Peace; we all need a bit of peace in our lives. I sit with this man and read for about two hours. There is something about reading the Bible on a quiet evening that just seems calming.

Just then he has family walk in the room. Two sisters came in with a few bags. When they see me sitting there reading the bible to their brother, they are overcome with joy! For about fifteen minutes they thank me for doing so. We stand there and have a nice conversation, then I quietly leave the room.

As I slowly walk down the hallway, I just think to myself that that was the best two hours of time investment that I had made in a long time! As I drive back home, I have the feeling that I will see this man again, in heaven!

Memorial Day kiss

I came in to our hospice today just after church service. My wife was working today, so instead of sitting around the house, I came in here to volunteer. That's a much better way to spend my time!

I walk in and make some coffee, do a little clean up and walk to the nurse's station. The nurses ask me to sit with an unconscious patient down the hall. I walk down the hall and enter the room.

In bed is a little old lady resting quietly. So, I announce my presence, so that she knows that she is no longer alone. I gently sit down on the couch next to the bed. I am there for about an hour. Just sitting there and making my presence known for the patient.

Then a couple of elderly ladies walk into the room. They are pleasantly surprised that I am there keeping their mother company. We have a wonderful and loving conversation for about fifteen minutes.

As I turn to leave the room, one of the ladies take my hand. It was a bit awkward for me and a surprise! She smiles at me and gently kisses my hand! She then says, "Thank you Father!"

She thinks that I am a priest! I try to tell her that I am not ordained into any denomination. She just smiles and tells me that I am her priest today! I just smiled and told her, "thank you." I let her have her joyful moment. And it was a joyful moment for me as well.

The Bible says that all Christians are priests of the Most High. I guess that that was my priestly moment! Being a priest or not, it is always wonderful to do a good deed for another. This lady was happy, and I was blessed forever!

I'm not ready to go!

I was at the hospice for a few hours already and I walk into a room with an elderly African American lady patient. She was lying in bed, as comfortable as the doctors could make her. She had battled throat cancer and was losing! Her condition was now considered terminal.

I walk into her room to see what I could do to aid in her comfort. I am just a volunteer with not much to offer, but I was compelled to try. Sometimes all we can do is to try.

She was lying in bed, and I could hear her breathing. She had a troubled look on her face! I introduced myself to her and told her who I was, and if there was anything that she needed.

She said something in a low raspy voice. I didn't hear her, so I leaned in real close. She kindly repeated herself. She whispered, "I'm not ready to go!"

I was uncomfortable in bring up the subject of death to her, even though that is what I thought that she meant. So, I said, "Go where?" I understand that may sound like a silly response on my part, but this was a very touchy situation!

She whispered again, "I'm not ready to go!" I then ask, "You're not ready to go, you mean dying!" She then nodded her head, "Yes!"

Now it was clear what she had meant. It sounds simple, but not to me. As a hospice volunteer, we are not allowed to proselytize, or preach a spiritual message of any kind. The hospice has chaplains for that type of need. The only thing that I could do was to walk to the nurse's station and to tell them that she needed the chaplain.

I lean into her and I tell her that I will let the chaplain know to come and see her. I do exactly that, and the nurse on duty for her already knew her need and the chaplain would be there soon.

In some situations, we can feel so helpless! Sometimes we can say something to help but are not allowed to do so. All we can do is to call the professionals and to say a prayer in private. Sometimes, all we can do is to give the situation to the Lord!

The Book of John

I came into our hospice an a very pleasant Saturday evening. The hospice was very busy this evening! There were a lot of patients and family members to talk too. I love it when it is busy and with a lot of folks to visit.

I had spent about three hours visiting patients and family members and doing some light chores. I was walking down the hallway thinking about leaving for the evening. Then just at that moment, I looked into a room.

There in an empty room, an elderly African American lady was lying in bed. I just stood there for a minute, observing the empty room! A hospice patient lying in an empty room is a very sad sight!

I then heard a voice say, "Go in and sit with her." As I entered the room, I felt the Love of God! I didn't understand why until I got into the room and saw the Bible on the table next to the patient.

I introduced myself to the lady and picked up the Bible. I noticed right away that it was the lady's personnel Bible. There was a marker at the beginning of the Book of John. It was right there, at that moment, that I know my purpose for the evening! I began to read.

I spent an hour and a half reading the Book of John to her. I read very slow and careful, just as the Bible should be read. The lady was unconscious, but I still think she could hear me read. They say that the sense of hearing is the last sense to go.

At first glance, I thought that that lady was in an empty room, dying alone! I realized at that moment, that no child of God dies alone! The Love of God was in that room, on that quiet evening. God was with her, and maybe there were angels in the room! I, a humble servant of God, temporarily, was also there in the room. She was not alone!

Action ministries

It was a beautiful Saturday morning at our hospice. I had just made some coffee for our guests. I then started to walk around visiting patients and family members. I was passing out mints as a way to start a conversation. Everyone would like a mint!

I walked into one room with an elderly man was unconscious and lying-in bed, and an elderly lady sitting in the chair reading a book. I introduce myself and offer her a mint. She smiles, thanks me, and take a few.

We started talking, and she tells me that when she and her husband had retired from their jobs, they sold all of their material possessions! I certainly don't hear of that every day! I told her that that was a huge decision to make and seldom does anyone do it!

This wonderful Christian couple took their faith seriously! I told her that and she laughed and agreed. They took all of the money and started a non-profit ministry called, "Action Ministries!" Action Ministries mobilizes communities to address the challenge of poverty, by focusing on hunger relief, housing, and education.

This ministry has been the work for years for them and their three children. This wonderful Christian couple was very happy that all three of their children has been saved through Jesus Christ and are working with them in their ministry!

We had a very nice conversation; they were very content with the condition of the father. They all knew that his life was to end here in this world, and a new life would begin in Glory! What a wonderful blessing! What a blessing to know that all of your children are spiritually saved!

Miracle on the sea

    I had just returned from a group hospice volunteer trip to the Holocaust Museum. I had popped into the volunteer office to review the current patient board. That is a board in which they have a list of patients, their age, ailment, and room number. Notes are added like, "no volunteers," or "volunteers requested," or "isolation," or pets requested.

    Some patients like to have visitors and volunteers. Other patients just want to be left alone. We have volunteers to fix the patient's hair or nails. We have guitar playing and singing volunteers. We have volunteers that give massages. We have folks that bring dogs and cats of all kinds, all specially trained for it. But most volunteers, like me, just come in to visit with the folks.
    I noticed from the patient board that the Vietnamese patient was still here and in the same room as last week. So,

I thought it would be a good idea to return for a second visit. I grabbed my badge and headed there. It was the first room on the right on the second floor.

I walked into the open door and said hello, the patient's daughter was sitting on the couch and immediately smiled when she saw me come in. She recognized me from last week's visit. The patient was still unconscious, and his condition looked the same.

She was very happy to see me and glad that I had come to visit her. She has been in our hospice for three weeks now and was very bored. She was happy to have some company.

Our first visit last week was a bit formal and stiff because she did not know me and therefor, she stayed a bit reserved. Now that she was now more comfortable with me, she was much more open.

After a few minutes she shared how her family arrived here. They were originally from the Republic of South Vietnam. She was born in South Vietnam in nineteen-fifty-nine. Her childhood was a life of continued violence in her war-torn country.

In nineteen-seventy-three, the American Army evacuated the country, and South Vietnam was on its own. Two years later, North Vietnam invaded the south. The South Vietnamese Army fought back but soon started to run out of ammunition. The United States, for political reasons, refused to resupply the South Vietnamese.

Low on ammunition and overwhelmed, the South Vietnamese Army fell back, and the Republic of South Vietnam collapsed and was conquered, by the communist North!

This kind lady before me was only sixteen years old at that time. Her and her immediate family decided to flee the country. Other members of their family had a small fishing boat available and helped them escape in the middle of the night! It was a very scary time for everyone!

They sailed in the night into the open ocean. There they encountered a larger ship. They were at first overjoyed, they thought that they were getting some help! They soon discovered that they were pirates! With so many people fleeing, the pirates in the South China Sea took an advantage of the chaos!

Her entire family were Catholics, so they started praying when the pirates took hold of their little fishing boat! They thought that they would be raped, murdered, or kidnapped and sold into slavery! She was a sixteen-year-old girl and was afraid that she would be raped and sold into slavery, and her family murdered! That is what the pirates had been doing!

She said that her Catholic family were praying as the pirates came aboard. Their prayers had a big effect! The pirates took all of their valuables but did not harm them. They even gave them food and water and directions to Malaysia! Prayer works!

The family made it to the country of Malaysia where they lived in a refugee camp. There, they all received refugee status and was allowed to come to the United States, where they all live today.

When the family was escaping certain death or imprisonment, they were guided by unseen forces, and a way was made out. When they were captured by the pirates, unseen forces protected their lives and kept them out of harm. It was clear to them the Holy Spirit was moving and protecting them along the way. Prayer really does work!

Around The Hospice

Holocaust museum

Back in the day, about eight to ten years ago, we had hospice volunteer meetings for team bonding. They were always very fun, and it was a good opportunity to mingle with other like-minded volunteers. We always had a good time, and it was usually coupled with an activity.

We all got together on a Saturday morning at about nine in the morning. We had a lunch and learning meeting. That means that we got together to learn about Jewish Wills. And the cultural significance of them. After that we ate our sack lunch that we brought with us. That's why it's called a lunch and learn; a lesson and a sake lunch afterwards.

After the class on Jewish Wills and our sack lunch in our back garden, it was time for our activity. This time it was a short trip to the Holocaust Museum, which was only about a mile from our hospice. Coupling the class on Jewish

Wills and the Holocaust Museum was a beautiful combination.

Our Supervisor of Volunteers who had arranged the Lunch and Learn is Jewish herself. So, it was fun learning and personal for all of us. It was very personal for our Volunteer Supervisor, and for us as well because we all loved her!

We carpooled to the museum because it was very warm outside. It was now in the afternoon. We arrived there and joined as a group by the front doors of the museum. We all had a guided tour waiting on us.

They had a few authentic "Star of David" patches that Jews were required to sew on their clothing. They had several short films and a lot of pictures. Outside, in the back of the museum, they had a replica rail car that was used to pack Jews inside to transport them to the death camps.

After the tour was over, at the exit was two Holocaust survivors! We all crowded around them and asked questions. I was absolutely speechless to be standing with two survivors of one of the largest mass killing in world history.

Going to a museum such as that is very educational and very eye opening at the same time! It makes you think about humanity, and how cruel mankind can treat others. It is polar opposite of our mission at hospice. The Nazis treated people in an undignified way. At hospice we do the opposite, we dignify the last days of people. I very much like the side that I am on!

Christmas decorations

The first thing that I noticed when I walked in our hospice was the Christmas decorations! None of the outside decorations are up yet, but they will be soon! Christmas is a special time at our hospice. We put up a lot of lights and trees to make the holiday special for our visitors.

After making some coffee and a few chores, I talked with the nurses on the first-floor nurses' station. They said that they had put up the decorations inside. More will be put up, usually by volunteers. Our volunteers love putting up the decorations! The maintenance man always puts up the outside decorations.

I noticed an elderly black gentleman sitting in the corner of a patient's room. So, I walk in to visit with him. He was the cousin of the patient lying in bed before us. He said that they had lived close together growing up, and they considered themselves as brothers. They grew up and played and went to school together.

Just at that point, the nurses came into the room to turn the patient, so we walked together to the break room. There, we talked about their church and his neighborhood. He had such great memories of his cousin. It was a great feeling to have him remember and talk about it. That's the spirit of hospice.

After I left him, I spoke with the nurses for a while. One of the nurses was stiff from putting up some of the decorations. I noticed a patient was asleep and alone, so I walked in and sat with him for about an hour.

At Christmas time people think of exchanging gifts. My gift is to provide compassionate friendship to the lonely and heart-broken people around me at our hospice.

A morning walk in the garden

I went in to volunteer this beautiful Saturday afternoon. It was very slow here today. That means that there is no one to visit with. The patient census is low, and the few visitors we have are in closed doors. If the rooms door is closed, I do not go in, my thinking is that they want some privacy.

So, I decided to take a stroll through the garden. Our hospice has a large, beautiful and well-maintained garden. The front of our hospice is nicely landscaped, and the garden is in the back of the hospice, it is walled off for the security of our patients.

It's a great place for patients and family members to get a peaceful change of scenery. They can go from a patient's room to a restful garden. We sometime even roll out a patient to enjoy the outside scenery. We only do that if medically we can do so. They absolutely love it!

Our garden reminds me of the song, "A walk in the garden with Jesus." I am a firm believer that every hospice or hospital should have a garden next to it. Around our spacious garden there are many benches, trees, bushes, flower beds, and stones. All of them have been donated by family members who have had a loved one here. Our hospice is a non-profit and this is one of the ways in which things are built, like gardens.

The garden is the perfect place to take a mental or an emotional break from what is happening inside. You can walk around, or just sit on the bench and watch the fountain, or the squirrels play in the tree branches.

Whenever I need a break from things, I know that I can just walk out the back door and take a walk around the garden. It's especially important for our family members, especially if they have been our guest for many days. Whenever I think about heaven, I always think that it would be like a morning walk in the garden.

The angel with a guitar

It was a beautiful Saturday morning at our hospice. I came in and made coffee and muffins for our guests. Afterwards, I walked to the nurse's station to see if I could visit with someone. They were overjoyed to see me! They did indeed have someone for me to sit with. A baby!

We had a pre-mature baby in our care. The baby was born with a tiny brain! Among the many medical problems this poor little baby was suffering, was its inability to suck! That means she could not feed herself from a bottle. They have to use a feeding machine, with a tube going to the baby's stomach.

All of the nurses love the babies that come into our care. That was certainly testified by all of the new baby clothes bought by the nurses and laid out on the bed. The issue the nurses have with the babies is that they need constant watching and attention. That would be no problem if that was all they had to do. But the nurses have a whole floor of patients and family members that also need their attention. That's where the hospice volunteers' step in to fill that need!

One of the favorite things that I love to do is rock the babies that are here. If there is anyone that is need of loving attention, it is the babies! That was my job to do for the nurses this morning. I was to rock the baby to free up the nurses, so they could care for the other patients.

I sat down in the rocking chair, put a pillow under my arm, and the nurse gently put the babe in my arm. When the baby was settled in, the nurse started the feeding pump. The feeding machine for babies, is a small machine on wheels, and they can put a feeding bag in it. Then it is slowly pumped into the baby's stomach.

While the baby was half done feeding, a beautiful middle-aged lady with long auburn hair came walking in the room. I had seen her before but didn't quite remember. She didn't come empty handed; she had a guitar in her hands. She was one of our volunteers who visited folks here and sang children's songs.

She was an amazingly friendly lady and a joy to be with. She sat down next to the baby and me. She put her guitar on her lap and started to play a song. Her playing was nice, and she had an angelic voice. It was very obvious that she loved what she was doing and understood the blessing she was sharing with us.

While she was playing and singing to the baby, she had a beautiful smile on her face and a soft glow about her! For a few minutes I thought that she was an angel with a guitar! She asked me if I had any requests, but I just told her to just keep doing what you are doing. She was certainly an angel with a guitar for this wonderful baby!

The feeding took about a few hours, but I rocked her for four hours! I called the nurse when the bag was empty, she came immediately and disconnected it. About every thirty minutes I would change arms. The pillow under the arm is a lifesaver! There is nothing better than a quiet room and a baby to rock! For whatever reason that I don't know, in those moments I feel close to God. I certainly felt close to God on that day!

The overcoming volunteer

I arrived at our hospice on a warm but cloudy morning, it was very muggy after all of the rain we have received this week. I went to the break room for a few duties and I found a new volunteer sitting at one of the tables.

He was in training, or I need to say re-training. He was an older gentleman, retired from his job, and a little chubby. He was here wanting to make a difference!

He was all by himself in the break room watching television, and he was having a little problem with the volume.

He was by himself because everyone else in the training class was at the funeral home doing a training tour. He told me that he had to bury two of his three children and didn't want to take that tour! He said that he had seen enough of that stuff!

I sat down with him, and he told me about his surviving daughter and his four grand kids. That was the family that he had left, and he was grateful for them!

He lost a son to a car accident, and a daughter to a disease! She was at our hospice in her last days, and he said that she received excellent care here. That's why he now wanted to volunteer here.

We then talked about my job and his desire to do something part-time. He had too much time on his hands and was a little bored.

He said that he was interested in volunteering for home care. I told him that since he was retired and had a clear schedule, that he was ideal for home care volunteering.

I was truly amazed on how strong this man was and the way that he was using his grief to motivate himself to do good things for other people, and to help them through their grief! He is a true over comer!

Nurses helping each other out

    I was at the nurse's station with another long-time hospice volunteer, A middle-aged lady named Anita. The Charge Nurse told us how another long-time nurse's aide, "Marie", who was a ninety-six-years old Hispanic lady, needed some help.
    She had just recently come down with a bad case of pneumonia. A case of pneumonia is always a concern, but when you are ninety-six years old, it's an emergency. That condition can easily kill you!
    Now Marie was an old crusty Hispanic lady with a continuous bad attitude. She was a lot better once she knew you, but even that took a few years! Her fellow hospice nurses were the only one who could work or put up with her. They were her only family. I guess that is why she was ninety-six years old and still working.
    Marie didn't have to work, she owned three houses and had plenty of money. But she was estranged from her family and had no friends. She lived like a hermit and would never allow anyone to know where she lived much less to come to her home!
    Even though this ninety-six-year-old nurse's aide had pneumonia, she still drove herself to her doctor's office by herself! Her doctor immediately called for an ambulance to take her to the hospital!
    But now that she was in the hospital and in serious condition, she was desperate enough to ask for some help. She asked the Control nurse to pick up her car at the doctor's office and drive it to her home. Marie gave up the keys of her car and her home to her friend at our hospice, a fellow nurse.
    To most people this situation would not be a big deal, but for Marie, giving those keys to someone else was a very

big deal. Marie, the hermit was trusting in someone else for a change.

When Marie was backed into a corner by her pneumonia, it was her fellow nurse's whom she turned to for help. It was the nurses who in turned helped her in her need.

In the end the pneumonia won the battle for Marie! She died a week later! But it was nice to hear that one of her last acts was an act of trust to a fellow nurse.

The great mule story

I came into the hospice on a Saturday evening. It was very busy; Saturday evenings are usually always busy. In-between patient visits, I stood for a few minutes at one of the nurses' stations.

While I was there, I started to talk to one of our long-time nurses. She was an African American nurse in her sixties, but she didn't look a day older than fifty!

She told me how that she was raised on a farm in East Texas. She had a wonderful life being raised on the farm. They were poor and didn't have much, but she said that, "you never miss what you never had!" She said that they did have plenty of food and that her mother was the best cook in the world!

Her father had a mule that he used for plowing fields, pulling wagons, and any other farm duties. She told me that in that day using mules on the farm was still very common.

She said that her father used to say that his mule would work all morning until noon, then the mule would just stop working!

The mule would not continue working until one o'clock. Every day he would take a one-hour break, and always at the same time!

She said that no matter how hard her father tried to get that mule to work between noon and one in the afternoon, he would not budge! After one o'clock, then he would work again!

I didn't believe her because I have never heard of anything like that. She insisted that the story is true though!

I kind of thought about it and then remembered that my dogs know exactly when it's time to be feed! If I should lose track of time, they always remind me!

My dogs are very good at telling time. I found out later that dogs can smell the flora outside. Throughout the day and night, the flora outside and maybe inside, changes throughout the day.

So, being curious, I decided to email the story to the National Mule Association in California. Yes, there is indeed such an organization!

I asked them if this story could have been true. After about a week, they emailed me back and said that they have never heard of such a thing and said that it was probably just a funny made-up story!

A few weeks later, I found the nurse and showed her the email on my phone, and we all had a good laugh about it! But she still insisted that the story was true! The nurse is a good old country girl, I think that I will just go ahead and believe her!

Stories Of Compassion

His sister called

The last four weeks I had been rocking babies! That has unfortunately become my temporary routine. Unfortunately, because it is always sad to see a baby in a hospice as a patient! One of the baby's went home with her patents, and the other beautiful baby went home to the Lord.

After with visiting several folks, I then sat with a gentleman who was unconscious and alone. No one should be alone at the end of their life. So, I sat with him to keep him company. Even though the patient was unconscious, I still think that he knew that someone was in the room with him.

I had been sitting in the quiet of the evening, just enjoying the solitude for about an hour. Then the nurse glided into the room. The patient's sister had called the nurse at the nurse's station down the hall.

She lived in Arizona and did not have any money to travel all of the way here to see him in person. She had been very distressed that her brother was dying, and she could not be there.

But the nurse had a talk with her and described to her that the last sense we lose when we are dying, is your hearing. So, even though she could not be her in person, she could talk to him on the telephone. On the phone she could tell him all that is in her heart. When she understood that, she was very relieved and grateful for the opportunity.

That is why the nurse had glided into the room while I was sitting there with the patient. The nurse smiled at me and told me what was going on. The nurse took the phone receiver off of the base and made sure his sister was there. Then she held the receiver to the patient's ear. The nurse held the phone while the patient's sister told her brother how much she loved him, and to say a final goodbye to him.

We could hear her talking on the phone, but we could not understand what she was saying. The nurse was very patient and loving. I could discern that it was a joy for the nurse to perform this act of love for the patient and his sister. I was just sitting there as a spectator, but I felt so blessed to be there to witness this act of love between a nurse and her patient.

When the nurse left, I sat there in awe. It returned to a quiet evening in a quiet room. I sat there and was grateful for what I had witnessed and was happy for the patient. After about thirty minutes the same nurse returned.

The patient's daughter was now on the phone! The same sign replayed itself. The nurse went through the same motion, and she was able to say goodbye to her father. I was blessed a second time!

When the nurse had finished and left for the second time, I remained with the patient. It was back to being a quiet evening. I sat there in the quiet, thinking that his family could not come to see him, but I was there! I, unwittingly, was there in their place. I was there standing in the gap. Their presence was missing, but I could be for them. They provided the loving words, and I could provide the loving presence. I was honored!

100 Years

After two weeks away from volunteering at our hospice because of the Christmas holiday, it felt good to be back volunteering. I made some coffee in the break room and checked-in with the nurses.

I visited with an elderly African American lady who was battling throat cancer! She could not speak, but we smiled at each other. Sometimes words are not necessary. She was watching television, and so I just sat down next to her and watched with her for about thirty minutes. She seemed very happy that I was with her. I stayed until she received some visitors, then I politely excused myself.

I then went to another room and sat with a lady that was one-hundred-year-old! Her name was Sally, and she was a very sweet lady. She had been suffering from dementia, but it was off and on again. Today it was off, and she was very sharp.

I asked her about her childhood and up bring. She said that she was born in the year nineteen-eleven in Sioux City, Iowa. The airplane had just been invented four years prior! She had seen a lot of history in her life!

She was a young sixteen-year-old girl and the oldest of seven children when her father was killed in a farming accident. With her mother becoming a widow and having seven children to raise, she moved the whole family to Los Angeles, California. It was a big move to make, especially back in those days, but she had family there who could help her.

The family was very poor, and her mother worked long hours in a factory, and would come home and take care of her children. Sally was sixteen and she also worked a job after school to help her mother.

Because they were poor, they never had anything. On Christmas holiday there was never any gifts. They would just be together and have a nice meal. All of the money went for room and board, and food and clothes.

One Christmas evening after the kids were put to bed, her mother was sitting knitting socks. Sally had just cleaned up the kitchen. Her mother looked up and with tears in her eye's apologized for not supplying gifts for her.

Sally, heart-struck, told her mother that it was okay. I told my mother that the family was all together for Christmas, and that was the greatest gift! I told my mother that every day that she went to work, that was the daily gift to our family! They both hugged each other and had a good cry together!

A few years later, Sally fell in love with a young butcher. They moved to Houston, Texas to open their own butcher shop. Sally lived there the rest of her life. But she never forgot that one Christmas evening with her mother!

Those don't need to be closed!

It was a nice quiet evening outside, the air was warm and still. I had scheduled myself to volunteer this Saturday evening. My girlfriend wanted to go with me because she wanted to go shopping! She knew some shops that were in the area of town where the hospice is, and she wanted to check them out while I was volunteering.

She dropped me off at the front doors and drove off. I went in and made some coffee and put some cookies out for our guests. A few refreshments for our guests make a big difference. Anyway, that is only my opinion.

I started walking down the hall, I saw an elderly African American lady lying in bed in an empty room. I walked in and introduced myself to her. I quickly looked around and I didn't see any personal objects around. That is usually a sign of no family visitations.

She had a problem with her memory, I asked her about her family, she knew how many children she had, but could not remember their names! It distressed her that she could not remember, I assured her that it was okay. I worked with her on remembering her family. She had three children and six grandchildren. But she still could not remember their names. It's very sad to lose your memory!

We had a difficult conversation, but she enjoyed the company. She was born and raised in Dallas, Texas. She was here because for the last few years she needed to live with one of her granddaughters. I asked her how it was living with her, and she surprised me with saying that she didn't like her granddaughter very much! I tried to laugh that comment off, but she did not.

We chatted for a while longer and she enjoyed it. When it was time for me to leave, I noticed that it was dark outside. She had a room facing our back garden, but at night it is unobservable. So, when I got up and started to close the shutters on the windows. Most people like the privacy at night.

As I started to turn the knob, she snapped at me and said, "those don't need to be closed!" When she snapped at me to reopen them, I did. When they were back open, she was fine. If she had a reason to keep them open, she didn't tell me. Anyway, if she wants them open, then they can stay open!

Dealing with people sometimes takes patience. It always takes compassion! All people should be treated as Jesus treated people. Jesus always treated folks with love and compassion. We should follow His example!

Memories of a mentor

I had taken a long break from volunteering due to my wife's health. The urgent needs at home should be a priority for anyone. Even though I was ready for a long break, being back felt very good! After a while, the hospice starts to become your second home.

It was a nice evening here at the hospice, nice outside and quiet inside. I was directed to a room by the nursing staff to sit with a man who was a bit restless. He was unconscious due to medication, but restless. This is one of the many reasons that they need volunteers around to assist them.

I was sitting there for about an hour, talking to him a reassuring him that he is okay, when a man walks into the room. I quickly introduce myself and tell him why I am there. I am at this point thinking that he is a family member.

He seems glad that I have been sitting with him and eagerly asks me to stay longer. I accept his kind invitation. The two of us talking and having a conversation would be a soothing sound to our patient.

He says that he is a Mexican National from Puebla, Mexico. But now, he lives in a resort town on Mexico's west coast. He is a manager at a hotel there and he had thirty-six people working for him. He said that he has a very successful carrier in the hotel business.

He then told me that the patient was his mentor and that he owed his carrier and maybe his life to him! He said that the patient started and managed a large resort in Mexico, for a resort company. He then accepted an offer from another resort company to start and mange a new resort in the same town.

The man said that he began his carrier as an airport shuttle driver, and that he helped him move up from position to position. He taught him all that he knows of the hotel and resort business. He said that he owed his carrier to him. When he had heard that he was in our hospice, he dropped everything to come here and be by his side! This was his time now to give back!

He told me that his best memories are from working with him. I told him that the best gift that someone can give another is a memory, because a memory will last a lifetime! Wealth is not how much money one accumulates in a lifetime. It is how much love one accumulates. It is how much people have we lifted up and helped. It is how many lives we have improved. Memories of a mentor do last a lifetime!

Light complaining is good

I had come in on a Saturday morning to our hospice. When I arrived, I meet one of our fellow volunteers here. He had been a volunteer in the past but had experienced a serious medical problem. He had to quit while he regained his health.

When he returned, healthy and ready to go, he went back through the training process. He told me it was a wonderful experience to attend the training classes. He was able to readjust to helping others instead of receiving it.

After I left him, I went upstairs to check in with a long-term patient named Nick. He has been here for months now. He only has twenty percent of his heart working due to his cocaine habit.

I peeked into his room, and he was sleeping. So, I went around filling up the mint jars at the nurse's stations.

When I finished that small job, Nick was awake. Nick is a homeless man who lives in his car, until his heart attack sent him to the hospital. His heart attack was due to his long-term cocaine use. He injected the cocaine into his arms with needles because getting high that way was quicker. Unfortunately, that way also has given him AIDS and Hepatitis C!

Now that Nick was awake, I walked into his room and greeted him. I didn't have to introduce myself because by this time I had visited with him many times already. He would end up being with us for ten months. For hospice care that is a long time!

Nick had just finished his breakfast and had taken a fast nap. He was watching television now. He was also busy rearranging all of his extra items that he always collects. If he doesn't eat anything in its own container, like pudding, jelly, juices, and things like that. He will save them for later. This is a typical habit for a homeless person.

The one thing that I noticed today was that Nick was constantly complaining! I took this as a good sign!

120

Complaining comes very natural for Nick, so I took this as a good sign that Nick was feeling better today. Nick was in his natural zone.

Nick was complaining about the nurses stealing some of his extra stuff. They had told him he could not stockpile the extra foodstuffs. They said that it was against to health department rules and would have to throw it away. So, he was looking for places to hide all of his loot! Stuff went under the bed sheets, some went under his pillow, and some went in the drawer!

He then started to complain about the people across the hall. He accused them of letting the granddaughter run up and down the hall and causing a lot of noise. I had spoken to the child's mother a little earlier, and she was a very nice lady. I didn't tell him any of that though.

In all total he spent about an hour complaining about different things! It was not any kind of heavy complaining where he would raise his voice or anything. It was just low-key light complaining.

Most people would be annoyed by all of his bellyaching. But I understood that this man has three separate medical issues that will kill him very soon! He had a bad heart, AIDS, Hepatitis C! With all of the medications he is taking and his ailments, the compassionate thing to do is to just listen.

When people are not feeling very well, we have to be extra patient and just let them sound off. They are not feeling well and that has to always be understood. Sick people should be shown some love and compassion.

That's why I just sat there next to Nick and smiled and agreed with him as he made his many complaints. Sometimes light complaining is good, and Nick was having a good day today!

Two patients pass on!

    Sommer time is here, it was eight-thirty in the morning, and it is already hot outside! I walked into the hospice and retrieved my badge and reviewed to patient board. The board was full, we have lots of patients here. I also see that Nick; our longtime homeless patient is still here.

    I walk over to the break room to see about restocking it for the day. When I walk in, I see the cleaning lady making coffee and putting out cups. In a fun way, I said, "Hey, are you doing my job!" She is a very nice lady and she laughed about it. Its nice that everyone here believes that we are all one team!

    I go to the second floor to see Nick, but he is still sleeping. As I was going back to the elevator, I see one of our nurses go into his room to give him some medication. She has to wake him up to give him the pills, and he looks at me to tell me that he would be going back to sleep, so I move on.

    One of the nurses ask me to sit with a patient that has been very difficult today. I walk in and an elderly black man was sitting up eating ice cream. I walk in and introduce myself to him and ask if he would like some company. He briefly looks up and says, "no," in a very forceful and determined voice! Sometimes the most compassionate thing that we can do is to turn around and not be there.

    I walk across the room and to discover that the patient had just passed away. An African American man and two ladies are in the room with him and grieving. I stand with them and offer my condolences and leave to allow them some privacy. Sometimes compassion that you provide has to be quick!

    I go to another room and sit down next to an elderly man with a long white beard. He is heavily medicated and lying-in bed. The nurse told me that he is a homeless man and has no family around. I sit with this man for about an hour.

Even though he is unconscious, it's always good to spend some time with someone who has no family present. I introduced myself to him, just in case he could still hear, to let him know that I was there with him and that he was not alone. Nobody should be alone in their last days of life!

After about an hour of sitting with our homeless guest. I go back downstairs and discover that another man had passed away! The man who passed this time is a Hispanic man with a large family present. I just stopped briefly and gave my condolences to one of his sons, a man in his fifties.

I think that this is the first time that two patients have passed away while I was present. Normally, I hear about it a lot, but after the fact!

I pass by Nick's room and peek in to see if he is awake yet, and sure enough, he is indeed. I sit with him for about an hour, watching television together. He said that breakfast was good, but he was not too impressed with lunch, which was a tuna fish sandwich and a bowl of soup. The cook walks in and Nick asked for some cereal instead!

So, my crazy day kind of ended with a very surreal feeling. Here is Nick, a homeless drug addict, turning up his nose at some very good-looking and smelling food. At the same time, two men had just passed away, and most of the other patients are close to death.

But it is not my job to judge others, that is the job of our Maker. My service to mankind here is to offer help and compassion to others, regardless of where, and what condition that I find them. That is what hospice volunteers do regardless whom they may be helping!

Hospice pain

I was in a room with an older lady and her son. They come from a family of Czech ancestry in the Shiner, Texas area. The older lady was the patient, she was in her nineties, and her name is "Polina."

Polina was kind of the quiet type and seldom said anything while her son and I spoke most of the morning. But there was another reason why she was so quiet. She was fighting a battle with pain!

She had cancer that was wrapped around her spine and was squeezing her like a boa-constrictor! Because the cancer was in and around her spine and causing a great deal of pain.

Her son, John, was very dutiful, and was very devoted to his mother. He had just excused himself for a while to speak to her nurse about her pain management.

The nurse very quickly arrived in the room with some oral medication. Polina took the pain medication, she pursed her mouth, and said that it tasted nasty! The nurse had a container of fruit juice in her hand and gave it to Polina. She drank it and washed it all down.

Most of the pain medication in hospice care is very strong because the pain that is being dealt with is very strong!

Some of the medication is injected into a peg tail or is given in a slow drip IV. Most of the time it is administered by a nurse, but sometimes they give the patient a trigger so they can administer the doses themselves.

The main mission of hospice care is to make the patients, who have very complicated medical conditions, comfortable in their end-of-life transition!

Different drugs are sometimes used together in order to be able to make the pain subside. The hospice nurses and doctors are very skilled at arriving at this very careful balance. They do this in a very loving and caring manner. Pain relief is one thing but doing it with a loving attitude is what a hospice team is all about!

Stories about The Babies

Goodbye sweet little baby

When I drove into the parking lot at our hospice, I noticed that something was going on inside. That's because it was hard to find a parking place! That is always a good indicator that a memorial service was going on in the chapel.

I walk into the front doors and talk with the security guard. He confirmed that a service was going on in the chapel and that we had a couple of very large families here! I always enjoy hearing that we are busy. That means that the patients have family visiting them and I will have lots of people to talk with and to help!

After making coffee and helping in our busy break room, I walked to the nurse's station. That's when I heard the news that a baby patient had just passed away in the loving arms of one of our wonderful nurses! When the baby passed, the nurse, who had been rocking her said, "goodbye sweet little baby!" It was sad news that the baby had passed away, but kind of a relief that the baby's suffering was over. That's the mixed feeling of being in hospice care!

I had a building full of patients and family member, so, I had to push onward. After taking an emotional break, I started to visit with families. We were so busy that day!

After visiting with many folks. I sat with a Vietnamese lady that I had visited with last week. She was happy to see me again. I guess she has been getting bored, since she has been here for several weeks already.

We talked for a couple of hours about her husband, whom was the patient. They had meet and married in Viet Nam during the war. After the Communist takeover of South Viet Nam, it was very chaotic. When the Communist took control, they people started to suffer oppression. They escaped by boat to the Philippines, and eventually made it to Los Angles, California.

As I was leaving for the evening, I was walking through the parking lot, and heard the sound of a goat! I walked over to a pickup truck, and sure enough, in a cage on the pickup truck was a goat! Now, that was certainly something different! This is a big city and very diverse, I guess I should expect anything by now!

I'm sharing this day of volunteering at our hospice just to relate how different people and their situations can be. In every room at our hospice is a completely different story going on! I often take a small break between rooms to mentally process things I seen and heard. In every room is a different person and a different story. Some of these stories are good, some are bad, and many are sad! But in every room a hospice volunteer shows love and compassion, and above all, understanding!

Baby rocking

The first thing that I noticed as I walked into our hospice was the first-floor hallway partition doors were closed. That means that someone has passed, and the funeral home folks are there to remove them to their funeral home. They do that for privacy for the family. They also discreetly use the back-utility elevator if they are on the second or third floors.

So, I went upstairs, and they were very happy to see me. As I approached the nurse's station, they eagerly told me that they had a baby. She was a little baby born to a Nigerian couple. The baby was the patient due to complications of a pre-mature birth.

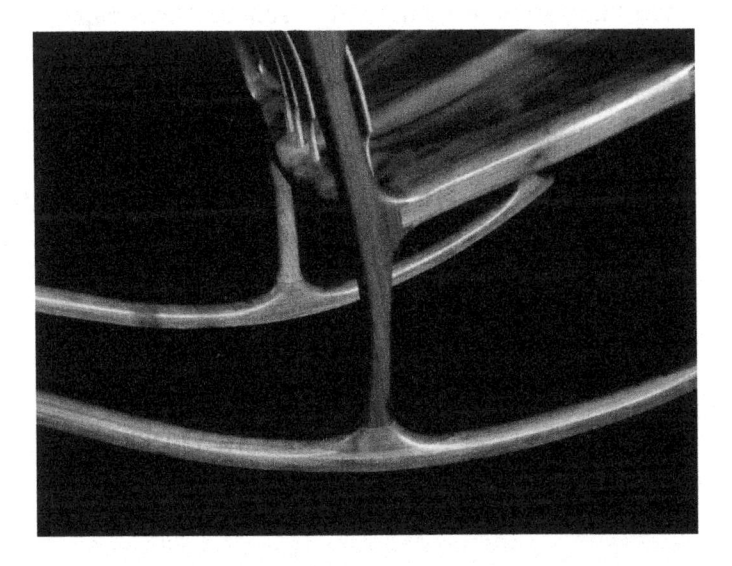

The baby was tiny! The nurses had her in a baby bed sitting on the desk of the nurse's station. That is where they could watch her better. They were smiling at me because I was about to free up a lot of their time so they could take care of the other patients.

They informed me that her room had a rocking chair in it. They picked up the baby and put her in my arms. I slowly walked down the hall to her room. They always give the back rooms to babies because they have a camera in the room, where they can watch the baby by camera.

She was such a good baby! I sat down on the rocking chair and put a pillow under my arm. I rocked her for four hours! Afterwards, I thought that my arms would fall off! It was a nice quiet evening, and in the back room it can get very quiet. Soft lights and a quiet environment, I really enjoyed it, so I just kept rocking away!

After four hours, the Nigerian family came into the room. When they had seen me rocking their baby, they were overjoyed! They were very happy to see someone giving their baby some love in their absence. I was happy to be of some service to them and to show some godly love to the baby.

It's always a blessing to show godly compassion to others. During the earthly ministry of Jesus Christ, he had always encouraged the children to come to him and he was always blessing them. He did that not only because he loved them, but to show us an example of how we are to treat children.

Baby strolling

Normally I volunteer at our hospice on Saturday afternoons. But my wife was off work that Saturday and she had to work on Sunday. So, I decided to go in to volunteer on Sunday afternoon, after church service.

When I went in, I was told by one of our wonderful nurses that a baby was here. She wasn't a new baby, but one that has been in and out of here on respite care five or six times already.

Respite care is when the parents need to have their loved one here while they go out of town, or just need a break from constantly providing care. This baby was one of these patients. To me its all the same, what I do doesn't change.

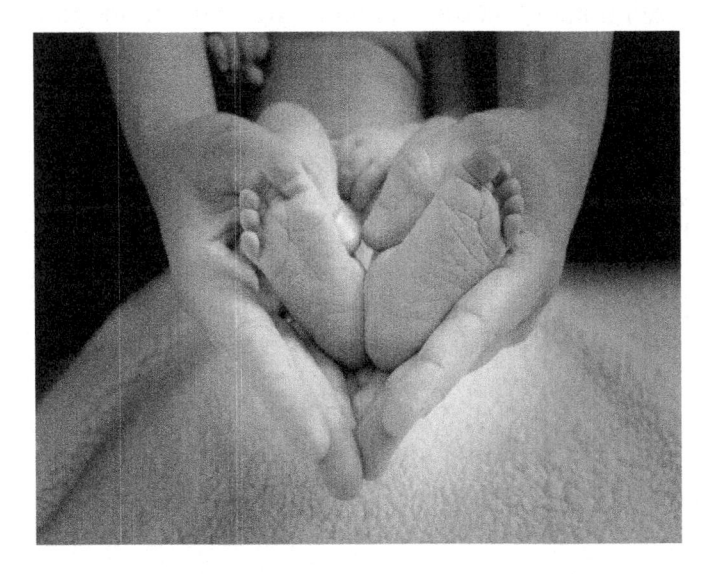

The nurse smiled at me and said that I was just in time for her feeding. We walked to the room, and I sat down in the rocking chair, put a pillow under my arm. The nurse took the baby out of her crib and gently gave her to me. She had her bottle all ready and gave it to me.

I nursed and rocked her for about an hour. It's a great thing when I'm not in a hurry, I can just sit there and let the baby nurse from the bottle slowly and at her pace. I nursed her until she dosed off to sleep.

I was there rocking her when the nurse came in to check on me to see if I needed anything. She pointed to the stroller sitting in the corner and asked if I wanted to push her around while she slept.

I thought that was a great idea! The nurse put the baby into the stroller, and I was on my way! I went slowly up and down the hallway. I strolled her for about thirty minutes.

She didn't finish her bottle before, so I sat back down into the rocking chair and let her finish. After about forty-five minutes, another volunteer walked into the room. She was there to relieve me so she could rock the baby for a while.

Whenever we have a baby in our hospice, we all flock to them. We all love to rock the babies. Not just volunteers, but the nurses as well, when they have the time. It's the volunteers though that will take turns to provide the love. If only we can take turns to provide love for everyone, this would be a much better world!

The untouchable baby

When I came in this Saturday morning to volunteer, I was told that we had a baby. The nurses told me that because of the baby's disease, no one could touch him! I went straight there to see about things. If anything, I could say some nice soothing words to him. I think that it's the babies that need the love the most!

I walked into the room and saw the baby in his crib. Sitting next to him was an elderly lady. She was one of our volunteers. Our volunteers have been taking turns staying with the baby, so that he would not be alone.

I was happy to see another volunteer. She was not ready to leave so I sat next to them. She told me that the mother of this baby has Downs Syndrome and lives in the States custody in a State house.

For people who have a mental illness of condition, the State have homes around the state, and are staffed by health care workers. It was one of these workers that raped the mother, who had Downs Syndrome!

The rapist is now in prison and the mother is not competent to be here! The hospice volunteers decided to fill the gap! We scheduled ourselves so that this baby would not be alone! Because of the baby's condition, he would not live long, hours to days maybe!

The other volunteer and I sat and visited for a little more than two hours. We talked about her life and her spiritual issues. In between we would talk to the baby. The situation for the baby is dire, but we created a beautiful environment for the few hours that the baby had left.

The next day this beautiful baby boy passed away! He returned to the loving God who blessed us with him for a time! Someday, when it is my time to pass away, maybe I could see this baby again. God has a plan for all of our lives, sometimes that plan is terribly brief.

Monday baby time

    I came into our hospice and a beautiful Monday morning. My usual day is Saturday, but I had to work last Saturday, and I could not come in. So, Monday is my day for this week. I especially wanted to come in today because we had a baby in our hospice. In order to give this baby lots of love and attention, we, the hospice volunteers made a schedule to rock her! I just cannot think of a better way to spend a Monday!

    When I arrived and retrieved my badge, I walked over to the nurse's station to find out the current situation. The nurse on-duty there told me which room to go. I walked down the hall and into the room.

    Another nurse was rocking the baby and finishing up the morning feeding. She was happy to see me arrive because she had her other patients to attend. She was enjoying her time with the baby, all of our nurse's love holding the babies that come here.

The nurse gently gave me the baby. A beautiful Asian-American baby girl! Unfortunately, she was born with very serious health problems that is cutting her beautiful life short.

I sat down with her in the rocking chair and made sure that the next two hours was filled with love and attention. She had a full belly and peacefully slept in my arms. I cannot think of a better way to spend two hours!

I rocked her while she slept until another volunteer arrived for her scheduled time with the baby. It was a volunteer that I seldom see, so I visited with her for a while, while she settled in with the baby.

It was a blessed two hour for me and hopefully I had given the baby a peaceful few hours. Jesus has told us that if we want to serve Him, then we need to serve the least of this world. I hope that today I did that a little bit!

A baby forever

I went to volunteer at our hospice on a hot and sunny morning. The first thing that I did was to check out the break room. It was out of everything! So, I spent some time in restocking the utensil's, cups, and making caffeinated and un-caffeinated coffee. It's always important to treat our guest well.

After that was all done. I immediately went up to the second floor. There was a baby here on respite care. Because the baby was born with a tiny brain, she was a year old, but still had a tiny body, the size of a new-born! She was so very small!

The baby girl herself was so cute and had the most beautiful hair! The reason that I had come up was to rock her. But when I arrived in the room, I saw that she was asleep. Rule number one with babies is that if they are asleep, don't wake them!

She slept all morning, so I didn't have the opportunity to rock and feed her. Maybe she will be here next week. I do not understand her future with her medical situation. I don't think that she has very long to live. She is destined by fate to be a baby forever!

Love without limits

As soon as I arrived at the hospice this morning, the nurse's let me know that there was a baby on the second floor. They all know that I love to rock the babies when they are here.

Whenever we have a baby here at our hospice, the volunteers schedule themselves so that a volunteer is available to attend the baby. Not only is it a big help for the nurse's but we enjoy sharing our love with them.

I walk into the room and another volunteer was there sitting with the baby. She was a baby that was born premature to Pakistani parents. She was born premature which caused the baby to have a bad heart!

When I arrived, it was time for the other volunteer to leave, so it was great timing. The nurse handed me the baby and I sat down on the rocking chair with a pillow under my arm.

I start rocking while the nurse continues with her other duties. The other volunteer hangs out and chats with me for about fifteen minutes.

We were in one of the back rooms and it is nice and quiet back there. It was a beautiful morning, and some sunshine was shining through the window creating a soft glow in the room.

I rocked that sweet little baby for four hours! The nurse came by an gave me a couple of breaks in between. Four hours is a long time to rock a baby, but the time just flew by. At the end I thought that my arms would fall off!

But I enjoyed my time rocking her. The parents were coming to take her home on Monday, and the baby needed some love and attention.

The parents are from Pakistan and considered this baby to be a flawed and worthless baby. Not only because she was a girl, but because she had a bad heart!

In the Muslim world girls have little worth and handicapped children are considered a burden. So, they were going to give their daughter up for adoption. In the Islamic world love has limits!

For that reason, I wanted to show as much love to this special baby as I could. I thought that it was a great investment of my time! I don't know of a better way to spent those four hours then to spend it with this unwanted little girl, who will soon perish from her heart ailment!

In many parts of this wicked world, there are limits to the love that they are willing to share. Not here at our hospice! This is an oasis of love, and here there is love without limits!

Diversity Of Life

The Trucker

I walked in the front doors of our hospice still munching on a cookie. There was a student social worker standing just inside of the front doors signing people in. I told her that I was a volunteer and didn't need to sign in. That was the first time that that has happened.

I walked around the corner and opened the door to the volunteer office. I retrieved my badge and reviewed the patient board to find out who wanted visitors, or the ones who don't.

After making some coffee in the break room for our guests, I walked down the hall to the downstairs nursing station. They let me know that the baby that I rocked was still here.

So, I went upstairs with the intention of spending some more time with him. When I got to the room, I found out that the family was there already. I was not disappointed, it's always better for the family to be there instead of a volunteer just standing in the gap.

I turned around and left, happy that I was not needed there. I walked down the hall was an elderly African American man lying in bed, I walked in and introduced myself to him.

I sat down next to him and asked him what he had done for a living. He said that he was a truck driver. He had driven a truck for forty-five years!

In fact, he was working only just a week ago! That is when he found out his ailment. He went from healthy and working to a bed in a hospice in just a short week!

He brought up his forty-seven-year marriage to his wife. They were marriage for a long time, but it had always been a very stormy relationship. It was such a bitter-sweet relationship that didn't bring him any joy.

After a brief scan of the room, I didn't see any personal belongings around. That's a good indicator that he has not had any visitors. He seemed very alone.

I was saved a little when the nurse walked in to give him some medication. The break in the environment kind of lightened things up a bit.

When the nurse left the room, then Tony, our volunteer chaplain walked into the room. Tony talked to him about the love of God. He prayed with the man about eternity and God's love that He showers on us.

This trucker seemed very touched by the words of the chaplain. I was glad to see that he was able to receive some comfort. We all need a little compassion at the end of our lives!

We talked again for a few minutes until he started complaining that he was too hot. It was probably a side effect to the medication that the nurse had given him.

He asked me to take some of the covers off of him, which I did. It still was not enough, so I went to bring in his nurse again.

The nurse and the social worker came in and tuned up the air and took some more covers off. Because he was feeling uncomfortable, he asked me to leave.

I left the room and went out to the back garden for a while. This visit was a hard one for me! It was a sad and scary visit for me.

This man lived a full life yet no one seemed to care about him in his last days. It was scary because his disease was killing him so fast! I couldn't help to think that the speed of his passing was the Grace of God!

The Korean man

I had just arrived at our hospice, and I was putting out cookies and making some coffee in the break room. One of the nurse's walked into the break room giving a tour of the facility to an elderly couple.

After my duties in the break room were done, I walk around the corner down the hall towards the nurse's station. As I am walking, I peek into a room on the right and see an elderly man standing and leaning of his bed post!

Patients here are a fall risk, so I run to the nurse's station and alert his nurse that he was out of bed! She then ran to his room and gently guided him back into bed and kindly reminded him that he is a fall risk and must remain in bed. He was an elderly Korean man.

While the nurse was getting him back into bed, I went across the hall and visited with an elderly African American man. We had a very nice visit for about fifteen minutes until he received a phone call. That means it's time to excuse myself and leave.

By that time the Korean man was back into bed. I saw a need in that someone needed to sit with this man and keep in bed. I decided that it was up to me!

I walked back into his room and pulled up the wooded stool so that I could sit next to him. I soon found out that his English was very limited, but we managed.

He seemed to be very happy in having me get some things for him. That is never a problem, because it's a wonderful service to offer patients.

He asked for some beef broth. We always have plenty of beef broth because often here that is the only thing they can consume.

I walked to the nurse's station and got a container of beef broth and a straw. After heating it up I brought it to him. He was very thankful for it.

He then asked for some beef jerky which we don't have. It was kind of funny that a Korean man was asking for beef jerky!

We visited for a while and the nurse's aide brought in a nice fish plate for supper. When he had seen the fish, his face lite up. I stayed with him while he ate. He ate it all and he really enjoyed it.

After his supper he asked for a Texas cookie! I did check with kitchen, but we didn't have any Texas cookies. A Texas cookie is a very large oatmeal cookie. It's called a Texas cookie because it is very large. Remember, everything is bigger in Texas!

We visited for a little while longer until he received a phone call, so I excused myself. As I was leaving his room, I wonder why he had no visitors. He was a very nice man, and I enjoyed his company, but some things you just don't want to bring up.

I walked back to the break room, and I had a nice visit with a couple about the history of our hospice. I then did my paperwork and left for the day. But I often think about the Korean man that I was blessed to visit with that day.

The Chinese translator

The week before I had a new volunteer that was to shadow me, but we got our email messages crossed and she didn't come in. This Saturday we were having our volunteer appreciation party, and as I was sitting in the chapel she walked up and introduced herself to me.

"Sue" was a very nice Oriental lady, middle-aged and very proper and polite. She is very stoic and did not show much emotion.

The first part of the volunteer appreciation party was in the chapel and was a dedication to our recent death of our Volunteer Coordinator!

Her daughter was there, and it was a very sad, and we were all in tears talking about her kindness to others. Our new hospice CEO was there also and said a few words. He is a very respected doctor and the husband of one of our volunteers.

At the luncheon in the office, I had remembered that earlier I had come across a Chinese gentleman, one of our patients, in one of the rooms that could not speak any English. So, I asked Sue if she spoke Chinese.

She proudly told me that she was fluent in Mandarin Chinese, Taiwanese Chinese, and German. She was from China but had worked in Germany for several years.

I couldn't remember which floor he was on, so we ended up looking on both the upper floors and finally found him on the first floor.

When we arrived at the room, there was four young Chinese American folks there visiting with the patient. They were from her Chinese Christian Church. They were leaving and were very nice and polite.

Linda walked right in and started to speak with the patient! A few minutes later the doctor walked in, and she used her as a translator. Linda was awesome and did a fantastic job! They immediately signed her up as a translator for our hospice!

I am sure that it was God's guidance and His Will that this lady arrived for the party and was just in time to help our Chinese visitor at our hospice. God answers prayer!

The Persians

I was at our hospice and as I walked into the break room, there was a family gathered there. Soon after speaking with them, I found out that they were Persians.

Some of the family were from Southern California, and some were from Toronto, Canada. They were all Christians and had immigrated out of Iran just before the Islamic Iranian Revolution!

That time was a long time ago and they are well settled here in North America. But it seems they also at the same time have held tightly onto their language and culture.

I spoke with this family in the break room and later in their room. They were very friendly, but also very reserved and not too forthcoming. Maybe they thought that I was a spy or something!

The two groups really enjoyed where they were living. The elder man that I spoke mainly with was from

Toronto, and he could not say anything bad about the place. The thought that it was a wonderful city. I'm sure that it is indeed.

The family had been here for forty years already but were kind of acting like new immigrants still. It seems that immigrating from your country for political reasons to a strange place makes a very deep impression on the migrants.

They were well settled but not completely comfortable. It's kind of made me a little sad for them. They were home, but not really at home!

The Czech

It was a very busy day here at our hospice. Our census is full and we have a lot of family members visiting. That kept me very busy going from room to room and helping the nurses in their daily duties.

When it's so busy I make sure that the break room has plenty of coffee made and is cleaned-up in-between patient visits. That also gives me a few minutes to reflect of the last visit.

One of the visits was with an elderly couple. The man was that patient and was lying in bed quietly resting. His wife was sitting on the couch by the window.

I walked into the room, and we share smiles, and I introduce myself. She was a bit bored and was very happy to have a visit with me. I sat down next to her on the couch and got comfortable.

We chat for a while about her husband and his condition and how long he has been here. Then she started talking about genealogy.

She had a great genealogy story to tell me! Both her husband and her are of Czech ancestry. The Czech people are from either The Czech Republic, Slovakia, Czechoslovakia, or the older Republic of Bohemia.

She shared with me about her Czech ancestry. She did years of research and discovered her family tree. The area of Central Texas where her and her husband are from has a large German and Czech population.

Of course, they are really Texans now, but she did find out where and when they had immigrated here. Her family came here through the immigration port in Galveston, Texas.

Many thousands of immigrants entered the United States through the port of Galveston, which is a genealogist best kept secret. There is even in Galveston today a very nice immigrant museum and data base for a genealogist to use.

She shared with me the Czech community in the area are where they live. In her research she discovered her family now living in the Czech Republic!

This kind lady had written them letters to introduce herself and was even invited to a family reunion in the Czech Republic. She said that she went and had a wonderful time visiting with all of them!

I shared with her that I had known several people with Czech ancestry and that I have a co-worker that had himself immigrated from Czechoslovakia!

My co-worker was a Czech Communist border guard when the Iron Curtain was dividing Europe back in the day. He had made the decision to get out and cross the Iron Curtain. That was a very brave decision because if he had gotten caught, they would have executed him!

One day, while on duty, when no one was looking, he crawled underneath a railcar going to Austria! He hid his rifle underneath some bushes.

He was hidden under the railcar for hours while it traveled to Austria! Finally, when it had stopped, he got out and walked around hoping that he had made it across the border!

When he discovered that he was indeed across the border, he was overjoyed! He applied for asylum in Austria, then he moved to Great Britain for a while, working as a truck driver there.

After some years, he immigrated to the United States and moved to Houston, Texas. Where he settled, got married, and has been working for my same company for the last thirty-one years!

She enjoyed the story very much. It is a wonderful story. We had a very nice visit together and it did put a smile on her face and took her attention away from her husband's condition for a few hours. That was my main goal. Family members sitting all alone with their loved ones can be very difficult for them! I was happy if I could relieve her mind if for a few hours anyway!

The Seamstress

I walked past the room several times during my morning of ministry at our hospice. An African American lady was very busy paying bills. She was sitting next to her dying mother lying peacefully in the bed.

I didn't go into the room earlier because I had seen that she was very busy, and I had a lot of other things going on that needed my attention.

After a while, the lady took a trip to the break room for a cup of coffee for herself. When she returned to the room, I noticed that she was now free from her burdens.

I walked into the room and introduced myself as a volunteer and asked her if she wanted some company while her mother rested. She replied that a visit would be wonderful!

This lady was the patient's daughter. She told me a beautiful story about her mother growing up in Victoria, Texas, and later in Corpus Christi, Texas. When they lived in Corpus Christi, they lived right by the sea!

Her mother and father loved to fish! They loved it so much, that they fished all of the time. When they lived by the sea, they fished almost every day, when they lived in Corpus Christi.

Later, they moved to the Houston area, about fifty miles away from the sea. Then, whenever they would go fishing, they would always drive the long way, just to enjoy the car ride. She said that her mother loved a good car ride!

She shared with me that her father had been a cook at restaurants. Her mother was a seamstress for all of the local refined ladies. She said that her mother was not just a seamstress, but the best seamstress in any town where they lived!

She could make any dress that the local ladies wanted her to make, from simple day dresses to the most elegant ball dresses. She always had a dress to work on, especially for proms and some of the local dances and private parties.

No dress was too complicated or too elegant for her to sew. She made the prettiest dresses in town, and everyone knew it and kept her busy sewing.

If she had a dress to sew, she would measure the lady, make the pattern for the dress, sew up the dress, and have the lady try it on and make the necessary alterations so that it would be a perfect fit.

Her mother always had a waiting list to make a dress, and her dresses were the one's everyone wanted! Everyone knew that her mother made the best dresses.

Her mother only had one regret in life. The husband of one of her clients offered to help her mother start her own dress shop! But her father did not want to take the risk of starting their own business. So, it didn't happen, and she always regretted it.

This grateful daughter that I was visiting with loved her mother and father. She said that they all had a wonderful life together. She shared with me about her love for her parents and their blessed life together!

The Oil worker

It was a very busy day today at our hospice. I love it when it's busy because I have lots to do and a lot of folks to visit with and help out.

I walked into one of the rooms and there was a patient of about seventy or seventy-five years old. He had just finished his breakfast, and he was leaning back to relax a bit.

I came in and introduced myself. I asked him if he wanted some company for a while. He readily agreed. So, I pulled up the wooden stool and sat down next to him.

I asked what he had done for a living. He said that he had spent his whole life working in the oil fields. He working on pumps and compressors.

Those folks are called millwrights. For anyone who doesn't already knows, the oil business has a lot of pumps and compressors!

He spent decades traveling all around the world installing brand new, and used or refurbished pumps and compressors. He fixed them and moved them around. He built new plants and lines, he repaired old ones.

The oil companies that he worked for sent him all over the world. He spent time in Iraq, Saudi Arabia, the North Sea, Venezuela, and of course, last but certainly not least, Texas!

I visited with him for a few hours. We talked about his work and the care he was receiving at our hospice. He seemed very reserved about his personnel life.

From talking with him it seemed that he didn't have much of a personnel life. He never married and had no children.

In that kind of business everyone works long hours. I kind of got the feeling that life just passed him by while he was always working!

On the outside, it seemed that he didn't care about that too much. I think that on the inside it was much different! I didn't ask too much about anything personnel, I discerned that I shouldn't go there, so I didn't!

When the nurse came in to give him a sponge bath, I excused myself. As I walked away, I felt a little empty inside. Not for myself, but for him. I just felt that there was a place in his life that was empty!

The Wanderer

I came into our hospice to volunteer on a Saturday afternoon. When I arrived, the nurse's informed me of someone who I could visit with today.

I always enjoy hearing that kind of news when I come into volunteer. Because that always means that I will have an interesting visit!

I walked into the room and see a large middle-aged guy with a long bushy beard lying in bed. Immediately he looked like an interesting guy!

He had just finished lunch and his nurse was collecting his food tray and was leaving. I sat down in the chair next to his bed and facing him.

He was a lifelong homeless man by choice! He had lived in Northern Arizona with his mother. One day he was sitting in her front yard, and he said that he heard the voice of God say, "give it up!"

So, he sold off the few possessions that he had and then just started walking down the road! Thus, starting his life as a "Wanderer."

He was in his right mind, that lifestyle was just his chosen way to live. Most homeless people are mentally ill or are drug or alcohol addicts.

But this bearded gentleman was of a sound mind and drug and alcohol free. He just wanted total freedom to wander around the country as he saw fit.

Our society looks at homeless people as one large group. We call all of them as "homeless people." But that is not totally correct.

Drug and alcohol addicts call themselves homeless in order to get some money to buy drugs or alcohol. They will panhandle on the street corners or wash windows.

They do that to get enough money to buy drugs of alcohol. They call that, "going to work." They go to work to make their drug money, once they have their drugs, they get stoned for a few weeks at a time.

Homeless people who stay drug and alcohol free, call themselves, "wanderers." That's because they choose a lifestyle of wandering around the country. Plus, they don't want to be grouped in with the drug and alcohol addicts.

He shared with me how they survive on the streets without any money, how they get money and how to get free food and something to drink. He really gave me a good education!

He shared a lot of stories about his life on the road and the streets with me in the nine hours that I visited with him!

One story was a time that he was in the countryside of Oregon. He was with a Native-American under an overpass. They were camping there for the night.

They started a small fire, and the Indian had a small drum! They spent the evening banging the drum and singing Indian songs!

When the evening was over and they were retiring for the night, the Indian gave him the Navajo name of "water bird!"

When he got sick with cancer, he went to live with his brother in a little town about fifty miles north of our hospice. Now that his cancer is progressing, he needs round-the-clock care.

Our hospice took him on as a charity case, which is not uncommon for us to do that for the indigent. Even the poor should die with some dignity!

In the end, he concluded that people should forgive and love one another! I liked that thought, and I thought that his life, in the end, did in fact teach him a good lesson.

He learned this lesson in life at the end of his. Life always in the end, teach us these important lessons. It would be nice to know them at the beginning of life, but at least we learn them eventually!

The bloodhound trainer

It was a very busy Saturday evening today at our hospice. I had come in at around five in the evening and the place was full of family and friends of the patients.

After doing a lot of chores in the break room, I took a short break in the downstairs family room. A patient and his family came in to watch the Nebraska/Oklahoma football game on the big screen television.

We had a very nice visit together as we watched the start of the game. After about thirty-minutes, they had more family members come in to watch the big game. I made a graceful exit to give up a seat.

I walked over to the downstairs nurse's station, and they told me about a patient upstairs that probably would like a visit.

I took the elevator upstairs and found the room. The patient was asleep, but his son was there. I walked into the room and introduced myself. His father was asleep, but the son looked like he could use some company.

He turned out to be a very interesting gentleman. He worked as a bloodhound trainer and handler and worked with a police department now very far from here.

He was eager to have some company and he told me a lot of police stories. He took care of the police departments dogs and handled the bloodhounds when they needed to track a criminal suspect, or a lost person, or a child!

He shared with me how a bloodhound dog would work a trail. He said that if you could imagine a trail of talcum powder of the ground, that is what a bloodhound's nose would tell the dog!

Every time that I see a bloodhound on television, that is now what I see him doing. It forever changed how I see dogs.

Dogs are also very good at telling the time of the day. All of the outside flora changes their scent though out the day and the night! The dogs can smell that change in great detail!

That explains why my dog at home can very accurately tell me that it's time for his lunch! The watch in his nose knows!

Cocaine and needles

Here is another story about a patient that I have called, "Nick." In a hospice where the average stay is about a week, Nick was with us for ten months! Because he was with us for so long, I did visit with him many times, and did get to know him very well. This story that I have called, "Cocaine and needles," was my first visit with him!

I came in early this Saturday morning because we are going to have a volunteer appreciation party this afternoon at our hospice. It's always nice to see and talk with my fellow hospice volunteers.

I came in and saw a gentleman finishing up his breakfast. I walked into his room and introduced myself. He said that his name was Nick.

Nick is a middle-aged man that has long hair and a thin, but full beard and mustache. When the doctor popped in for a quick chat with Nick, she exclaimed that he looks more and more like Jesus every day! I remarked that it was an accurate description. Nick seemed amused by the comments.

Nick's amusement didn't last very long! Not long after the good doctor left, Nick's real mood came out! His mood turned a bit sour, and he started to complain about everything!

He complained that the nurses were not attentive enough and the food that was served was never enough! I was kind of taken aback by those complaints being that Nick is a homeless man, and not all of his needs are being provided to him free of charge!

I looked around and I noticed that he was stockpiling stuff. He was hording juices, left-over food, and lots of Styrofoam cups!

Nick is a homeless man, and homeless people commonly horde things like that in case they need it later. It's a survival trait that the homeless learn very fast when they are living on the streets!

Nick is suffering from AIDS and Hepatitis C, but he was dying from heart damage from his long-term drug use. He only has twenty percent of his heart that was working!

He was in the hospital for treatment, and they said at the time that he had forty percent of his heart working. When he was discharged, he went back to his broken car that he was living in and shot up some more cocaine!

Soon after sticking the needle in his arm and injecting the cocaine, he dialed 911 and passed out in his car! When the ambulance arrived, they had to drag him out of his car because he couldn't walk!

They brought Nick back to the same hospital and they told him that he now had just twenty percent of his heart working! He was mad about that because he had thought that the doctors at the hospital had lied to him!

I mentioned that it could have been that hit of cocaine he had injected into his arm. Nick looked at me like I was crazy, he said that it was just one hit.

He mentioned that his feet were now black from a lack of circulation! I acted amazed by that and told him that I have never seen anything like that. So, he uncovered his feet to show me! I was very much taken aback by the sight! Both of his feet were dark black!

His suffering from AIDS, and Hepatitis C, and his bad heart, was a direct result of his lifelong cocaine usage by using needles to inject cocaine into his body.

As the Bible says, we "reap what we sow!" I certainly didn't tell him all of that, but I'm sure deep down inside, he understood it!

Nick shared with me that he used needles to inject cocaine because it gave him a faster and better high! He had started his addiction by snorting it up his nose, but that in time tore up his sinuses! Once he started to inject it with needles, he never went back to snorting!

His cocaine addiction started as a small habit; it then became a bigger part of his life. Then he couldn't live without it.

His addiction caused him to fall behind on his child support payments on his three children. Then he lost his job in construction, because he was always stoned! When he lost his job, he moved out into the streets!

He wasn't getting any cocaine in the hospital or here in our hospice, so I was wondering how he was dealing with it so well. I didn't ask about that; I didn't want to upset him. Maybe they were giving him a drug substitute, I don't know!

Nick was on probation from the courts because of him not paying any child support. He shared with me that the Internal Revenue System was also after him for back taxes!

That's a lot of problems he was dealing with all because of his cocaine addiction! He had chosen over some time to sacrifice his entire life and that of his children, just to get stoned on cocaine. I thought that it was very sad. Not only for him but for everyone around him.

Nick was not a very nice person, but he was a product of his habit, so I did my best to visit with him and to treat him with respect. We all live in an undignified world. His world was a world of drugs and needles on the mean streets. I wanted to try and help provide a little dignity in Nick's last days!

Poems

A windy night

A windy night
blowing in the cold air
the temperature dropping
almost too much to bear.

A windy night
is when I think about you
the things you haven't said
the things you do not do.

I tried so hard to make it right.
I should have put up more of a fight.
I tried to protect you, to make it right.
With your mother, I didn't want to fight.

I sure do miss you
And love to have you in my sight

I'm just sitting here wondering
On a windy night.

I tried so hard to make it right.
I should have put up more of a fight.
I tried to protect you, to make it right.
With your mother, I didn't want to fight.

Frustration

My father is dead
My mother is a crack head,
Life feels so difficult
When you can't get ahead.

Frustration is building every day
I can't get a handle on life
I can't get a job
I can't get a wife.

Frustration is what I know
It follows me everywhere I go,
Life feels so difficult
When it drags on so slow.

Frustration is building everyday
I can't get a handle of life

I can't get a job
I can't get a wife.

My brother just plays video games
Games of killing and people maimed.
Life feels so difficult
All of it just feels the same.

Frustration is building everyday
I can't get a handle of life
I can't get a job
I can't get a wife.

For the sake of the rose

For the sake of the rainbow, in the rain we must mourn,
For the sake of the rose, we must water the thorns.

If life's trouble was an inch,
We would have a mile,
But all of it is worthwhile,
But for only a smile.

If life's heartache was an inch,
We would have a mile,

You would still make my life beautiful,
Like a lily of the Nile.

If life's strife was an inch,
We would have a mile,
You would make my life more pleasant,
Like a green valley on an emerald isle.

For the sake of the rainbow, in the rain we must mourn,
For the sake of the rose, we must water the thorns.

The rest of the way

We didn't get to walk down this road together,
but I will walk the rest of the way thinking of you.

I have tried to think how I could have been better,
love and hard work were something I always tried to do.

But,
we didn't get to walk down this road together,
but I will walk the rest of the way thinking of you.

You tried very hard for us not to be all together,
everything was destroyed and scattered as your anger grew.

But,
We didn't get to walk down this road together,
but I will walk the rest of the way thinking of you.

Sermon's preached to people and Bible's made of leather,
words of life ringing out to empty-headed people in the pew.

But,
We didn't get to walk down this road together,
but I will walk the rest of the way thinking of you.

In the end you left me dangling in the breeze like a feather,
delaying, unsure of what to do, thinking of the taboo.

But,
We didn't get to walk down this road together,
but I will walk the rest of the way thinking of you.

In the end, debating to myself and talking to others,
God gave me the release to leave and wish you adieu.

We didn't get to walk down this road together,
but I will walk the rest of the way thinking of you.

God's Love

Although I have turned away,
Your love is still in my heart.

Although I have fallen into sin,
Your Spirit had only begun to start.

I started slow and easy,
And I grew stronger.
My love increased and grew,
But over time my heart glowed no longer.

Although I have turned away,
Your love is still in my heart.

Although I have fallen into sin,
Your Spirit had only begun to start.

As the weight of life grew heavy,
Instead of turning to you,
I abandoned your Spirit,
And became a fool.

Although I have turned away,
Your love is still in my heart.

Although I have fallen into sin,
Your Spirit had only begun to start.

I awoke from my slumber in due time,
I dusted off my sword of the Spirit,
And put back on my suit of armor,
God's Glory helped me in rebuilding my merit.

Although I did turn away,
God's love never left my heart.

Although I was a sinner,
I now in Christ have a new start!

Stories of Human Struggles

The flowers are now blooming

I came into the hospice on a hot summer day. I had found myself with a middle-aged man. He was a construction supervisor. I am a truck driver and had worked a few years of construction, so we had a lot in common and understood ourselves.

Because we had a lot in common, we talked a lot of shop talk, which made him happy. I could tell that he put a great value on his profession. His job was the only source of stability in his life.

I was soon to find out why. He had no children, but he did have four ex-wives! That was of no big surprise to me because I could tell from the beginning that he was a type A personality! That type of personality is very hard to live with and to work for also. Their lives tend to be full of trouble!

Whenever I visit with someone, I tend to bring up past love lives and how they meet their spouse. With this gentleman having four ex-wives, that seemed like walking in a minefield! I left all of that alone!

He has a sister here in town who has been taking care of him. He has two other sisters who live out of town who he said that he, "didn't get along with!" I was not very surprised to hear it. With four ex-wives and an estranged family, he seemed to have lived a very stormy life.

So, I said to him that since he had nothing to do but just lay in bed, it might be a good thing to give them a call and see how they were doing, and to let bygones be bygones. I thought that the idea might have made him angry, to my shock and surprise, he agreed!

At about that time his lunch arrived. He really enjoyed his lunch, I don't blame him, our hospice produces great tasting food from our kitchen. We talked while he ate.

Just after he finished his lunch, a middle-aged man walks into the room. He is an old high school friend! The environment of the room instantly brightened up! They greeted each other with great excitement! Now we had a party going on!

Now that an old friend had arrived, I tried to excuse myself, since now I thought that I was no longer needed and now just in the way. Both of them insisted that I stay in the room. I sat back down and enjoyed their conversation.

They both happily talked about their high school days, growing up and weekend trips to the beach together. I had the same lifestyle growing up and visited the same beaches as they did grow up, so the three of us had a fun conversation together. The three of us told a lot of great stories about our teenage years and the fun and crazy things that we all did.

Then his sister and a nephew walked into the room. Not the sister that had taken care of him here in town, but one of the sisters that he was estranged from!

I was afraid that it would be an awkward meeting, but it was not at all. It was a joyous and tearful reunion from the start! They embraced each other and cried together, happy tears. All of the past issues just faded away without regret.

As they embraced each other, I quietly slipped out of the room. I now felt that my job there was done. I felt that I had stood in the gap in a short time before the joy started. As I quietly walked down the hall of our hospice, I thought to myself that even though this patient had lived a very stormy life, the flowers were now blooming in his life!

Indiana orphanage

Well, here I am, sitting with the same lady that I sat with last week. Last week we had a wonderful conversation. This week she is much weaker and unresponsive. I am sitting with her and reflecting on the physical change she is going through right before my eyes. Her disease is now progressing more rapidly!

I am sitting here feeling sad about her decline but feeling blessed that I was able to visit with her last week. It was a very awkward feeling. As time goes on, I am happy that I could spend a few hours with her.

Her nurse told me that her daughter is now with her. I was glad to hear that because last week she was all alone. I looked around the room and noticed an old stuffed animal on her bed, and a photo album and a white bag on the couch. Last week there was no one here. I'm happy to see that she has some family here now.

Her husband is in Florida I was told. He was also in declining health which prevents him from traveling to see her. She also has a son, maybe he is in Florida with his father. I don't know, but I hope so.

Last week we had a nice conversation. We didn't talk about her current family, or her carrier. Instead, we talked about her upbringing in the custody of the State. I did not ask about her parents, or the rest of her family, and why none of them could take her in, to be raised.

I perceived that it was a sensitive issue and stayed away from it, unless she brought it up, she did not. It's my job to bring up the good memories and stay away from the painful ones. With death rapidly approaching, the pain will soon be relieved!

This gentle lady was in two different foster homes as a child, until she was put in the custody of the State of

Indiana. I did not ask why the two foster homes failed, and she did not tell me, maybe she couldn't remember. But, regardless of what happened or why, she ended up in an Orphanage of the State of Indiana.

At the orphanage the children had a structured life. To most of us, that doesn't sound good. But to someone coming out of a life of chaos, it's a godsend. The children had a dormitory style life, it was efficient. They had schooling, chores, and rules. Discipline was strict, but with a lot of kids in one place, they had to keep it under control!

One of the things that the children did, was as they made their beds in the morning, they would tie rags around their feet, which would shine the floor at the same time while making the bed. Doing two chores at one time would add some play time at the end of the day!

Every Christmas it was a custom at the orphanage that the children would sleep with their feet sticking out from the covers. Because the meter man would go down the beds and hang candy canes on their toes! The meter man wanted to do something for the kids on Christmas, and that's what he did for them.

After she told me those stories, she asked me if we could go out to the garden. It was a beautiful day outside and I said that we sure can. I went and got the nurse to disconnect her. She was taking pain medications intravenously, so we could not go for very long, or the pain would start to return!

After unplugging her, I rolled her in her bed out the back door, and into our back garden. She really loved it! She had always loved the outdoors. After about fifteen minutes, I could tell that she started to struggle a bit. Ten minutes after that, she said that the pain was getting to be too much and wanted to return to her room.

I rolled her back to her room and hooked her back up to her pain medications. She was so grateful for that small amount of time in the garden. I was happy that I could do that for her. After a few minutes her physical pain subsided, and she could once again relax. One of my best memories is giving this lady thirty-minutes of joy at our hospice.

Last week it was a great visit for me. Today, as I sit here with her again, I am remembering the time we had last week. I quietly watch her resting in bed. The pain medications are keeping her comfortable, relieving her of the physical pain of cancer. But, sitting there, I understand that soon, death will free her from the emotional pain she had suffered all of her life.

A troubled man

It was late in the evening at our hospice. It was quiet and the lights were dimmed. In one of the rooms was a middle-aged man lying in bed and watching television.

I walked into the room and introduced myself. He kept looking forward at the television with a blank stare. Normally I would excuse myself at this point, but something urged me to stay! So, I asked him if I could watch television with him. He nodded yes and I walked around the bed and sat on the wooden stool next to him.

We watched television for about an hour. During the commercials, I would ask him questions to start a conversation. But he didn't seem interested.

He had never married and had no children. He did have a large portrait of a middle-aged man on the table. I discerned that he was gay. I didn't ask him! If I had it wrong, and he was not gay, it would have been insulting!

He was alert but seemed very depressed. I looked around the room and there were no personal items, flowers, stuffed animals, nothing! It appears that he has had no visitors. Only that one portrait, all by itself! I kind of got the impression that his partner had abandoned him to his fate.

I felt a sadness come over me as we finished his television show. When it was done, he abruptly asked me to leave, because he wanted to sleep.

I did not feel rejected. If there is one thing that I have learned is that I cannot please everyone. I was grieved that I could not help him in some way. The man needed compassion and I felt that I had a lot to give. He just could not accept it. I felt the spirit of depression in the room as I left.

He was a troubled man! I felt that I tried to help the situation, but we cannot win every battle. I left the room and prayed for him in the hallway. Some situations we just have to leave for God to handle.

Still going strong

I had visited with a middle-aged lady, who was the patient, and her husband, that had been in our hospice for the last three weeks. I saw her husband first in the downstairs breakroom and visited with him for about an hour.

Then, together, we both walked up to the room where his wife had been lying in bed struggling with brain cancer. We walked in and his wife was gone! Her nurse walked up and said that another volunteer and her went out to the smoke shack to have a cigarette, or three. She has been a chain smoker all of her life and would go often to smoke. In the last weeks I had taken her several times.

For someone who has been battling brain cancer for the last two years she looked good! Her husband said that she was even walking around a little bit on her own! This is not the first time she has been in our hospice ether. This is the third time that the doctors had assigned her here. Each time she would get better and could be discharged and return home!

The other weeks that I had visited with her she would even brag about the number of tumors in her brain! She would say that I have seventy tumors in my brain, and I am still going strong! She was a fighter!

While she was out smoking, her husband and I chatted in the room until they returned. Her doctor stopped by to see her while we were waiting. The doctor was a visiting Japanese doctor. She was here to learn to be a hospice doctor.

The volunteer she was with was new and inexperienced. She told the patient that she needed to stop smoking, because it's bad for you! That is something that a volunteer should never say! If a patient already has a terminal health issue, there is no use in stopping now! With a terminal illness, smoking is no longer a bad habit, but a comfort habit!

We all talked about it and agreed that her smoking is no longer a problem, but a comfort habit that she should keep doing. The patient certainly agreed and didn't want to quit.

She said that the joy she got out of smoking helped her along. She had smoked all of her life and it was a comfort in her life. I was impressed with her zeal for living and fighting the dozens of tumors in her brain. She had a great spirit and was a fighter, and she was very proud that she was still going strong!

Control!

    I went in the hospice to volunteer on a warm quiet Saturday evening. After getting my badge, reviewing the patient board, and other duties like making coffee and restocking the break room. I visited with several patients and family members downstairs, then I went upstairs.

    I went to the nurse's station to inquire about any patients who would like some company. She told me of a patient down the hall, who was in a great deal of pain. The nurse said that this lady might want someone there, but maybe not.

    The nurse continued and told me that the patient has refused any pain medication, even though she was dying of cancer! The reason was that she wanted to remain in control! As a patient, she has a right to refuse any medication. And that is exactly what she wanted!

    She told me what room that she was in. And then I walked over there. I walked into the room, and in bed with a clear hard plastic cover over her, was a middle-aged lady. She was shaking all over in agony, gritting her teeth, and squeezing the sheets until her knuckles was pure white!

    This horrible scene had made me very uncomfortable! I was uncomfortable because the scene was so terrible and there was nothing that I could do to help her, like I can for others. When I walked up to her, she looked at me, and I could see the agony in her eye's!

    I asked her if she would like me to sit with her. She shook her head "no!" I kindly replied "okay" and slowly left the room. It was a very awkward moment for me! I hate to admit it, but I was happy to get out of the room! To be in the same room with someone who is experienced extreme suffering was very disturbing!

I walked out of there with absolute amazed that someone would value control of her body and surroundings that she would go so far as to refuse medication! To choose to spend the last remaining days of your life in terrible pain because she valued control more! It was so hard to believe and comprehend!

As a Christian we learn to give up control to Jesus Christ. I think it is much better to let God, and others to have control. I have known many control freaks in my life, and I have always been disturbed by them. Because control over anything in this life is just a fantasy. We are really not in control of anything. God is in control, and we are just riding along in life. That night I renewed my faith in God to allow Him to have total control of my life!

Sadness overcame by joy

I had come into our hospice on a Saturday evening at about seven. I get up early every day for work, but I know that I am off tomorrow, and I can sleep in.

This evening I was being shadowed by a new volunteer! A young guy in his twenties. We had spent a few hours visiting with the patients and family member.

I was just showing him how I do things; everyone has their own routine on how they do things. I always restock the break room first, then check in with the nursing staff to let them know that I am there and available. Then I start to visit with folks.

We were walking down the second-floor hallway when I see a middle-aged lady sitting on the couch by the window. The window blinds are open, but it is dark outside, and it looks black. The rooms lights were off except for a couple of lamps, which made a soft glow in the room.

My shadow and I walk into the room and introduce ourselves to her. There is an elderly lady in bed next to her. I could tell immediately that she had been crying! Starting a conversation with someone who had been crying is always an awkward situation.

I asked her if she would like a little company for a while. With a soft quivering voice that cracked a little when she talked, she said that it wasn't necessary. But I sense that she does really need some company.

I paused for a moment, and then asked if the patient was her grandmother. She replied, with a small smile, that she was her mother. I already knew that, but I just wanted to give her an indirect complement to make her smile a bit.

When I mentioned her mother then she started to open up and to tell me about her. She said that her mother was a loving and compassionate lady! We talked about her and her whole family. I told her that the Hand-of-the Lord was on her family and that they had really been blessed.

At that moment, the nurse walked in to reposition her mother, so we stepped out into the hallway. There, in the hallway the three of us kept talking and enjoying each other's company. I shared my feelings that God had blessed her and her family to a great extent.

She paused and thought about that and agreed. She had always looked at things in a secular way, but she agreed that the Hand-of-God was upon her family. Looking at her family in that way filled her heart with joy!

When her mother's nurse had finished turning her mother, we went back into the room and continued talking. We visited for about two or three hours! By the time that our visit was wrapping up, this lady was smiling and beaming and full of joy!

As my shadow and I were walking down the hallway towards the elevator, I turned to him. I told he that that was the perfect visit here at our hospice. We walked into a room of sadness and left it hours later leaving an environment of great joy. I told him that these are the visits that I live for! This is what being a hospice volunteer is all about!

I have lived a hard life!

This next story I have saved for the last. It starts off very sad but has a hopeful ending. As the Bible says, "Though I walk through the valley of the shadow of death, I shall fear no evil, for thou art with me." That is just one line of the twenty-third psalm, but it tells me a lot about living life!

I had walked into the downstairs break room to make some coffee, when I met an older Hispanic man sitting in front of the television and drinking a cup of coffee. His name is "Roy."

When I got the coffee maker busy brewing, Roy looked over at me and said "hello" in a way that told me he wanted to talk!

He told me that he had lived a hard life! He was in the produce business, and he had to file for bankruptcy! His wife had died of cancer at the early age of forty-four! And because of all of that he had turned to alcohol and became a drunk!

All of that happened in the end of the last century. At the start of this century, he decided to change his life for the better!

So, he decided to move to the State of Arkansas because it was a dry state. I knew that that was not correct. Arkansas is not a dry state, but it does have several dry counties. That is probably what he meant, but I did not correct him.

He got a small job in a dry Arkansas county, and he didn't have a car, so he stayed in his apartment so he could dry out, and get off the bottle. He said that it worked, and when he was ready, he returned to Houston.

While he was drying out in Arkansas, Roy said that he lived in the hill country between Oklahoma and Little

Rock. Arkansas is half mountainous and half flat country. He said that the "highlanders" and the "flatlanders" in the area would tell jokes about each other. But he said that it was just friendly kidding!

Roy then shared with me that he had recently been in a truck accident. Several broken ribs and a punctured lung on his left side! He even raised up his shirt to show me the scar where they had to do surgery!

Roy said that after the accident, he was in a coma for a month. When he had woken up from the coma, Roy thought that he had just gotten to the hospital! The doctors and nurses had to tell him that he had already been there a month and would be there another two more weeks!

Roy most certainly had lived a hard life. But we continued to talk, and he shared with me that a miracle had just happened!

His mother was here at our hospice. Two weeks ago, both of her kidney's had shut down and were not working! Being that she was in her eighties, they considered it to be a terminal condition.

The doctors in the hospital sent her here to die peacefully. But God had other plans! When she arrived and after the priest gave her last rites, she got better!

Not only did she get better, but both of her kidney's started to work again! Everyone said that it was a miracle! Roy even said that they were thinking of letting her go home! Roy certainly had lived a hard life, but God shined into their lives in these late days just to reveal Himself and to tell them that He still loves them!

Regardless of the tribulations and challenges in our lives, God loves all of us. He loves us so much that He sent His only begotten son into the world to be a sacrifice for our sins and to make a way of forgiveness and salvation. No matter what kind of pain life inflicts on us, we will always have hope in Jesus Christ.

About the Author

William James Roop, M.A.B.S., has been a hospice volunteer for ten years with the same hospice. He is a graduate of Purpose Institute with a degree in Ministerial Studies. He is also a graduate of Apostolic Theological Seminary and Bible College with a master's degree in Biblical Studies.

He has had ministries in nursing homes, bus ministry, church librarian, church security, and teaching Sunday school classes. He attends the Church Triumphant in Pasadena, Texas. He has written one other book and a blog. He makes YouTube Bible study videos, and a new video series called "The Hospice Moment," which will be coming soon!

Book: The Basics of Biblical Hermeneutics, published by Kindle Direct Publishing. April 2019.

Book: Apostolic Church History, Volume 1. Published by Kindle Direct Publishing. April 2022.

Book: Apostolic Church History, Volume 2. Published by Kindle Direct Publishing. July 2022.

Blog: Hospice Care and Dying,
www.hospiceministryvolunteer.blogspot.com

Blog: The Bible and Life,
www.biblicalhermeneuticsposts.blogspot.com

Blog: The Trucking Tango,
www.trucksandbanjos.blogspot.com

Videos: YouTube Channel,
"Brother Roop teaches the Bible"

Videos: YouTube Channel.
"Bill & Gretchen's Tin Can"

Website: www.billroopministries.com

Notes